C000093978

"Anyone who has worked in the ministries of wor to invest into the spiritual lives of those entrusted t book does that, and more. Wally Horton brings mor ence as a church musician to these devotional writi formational, spiritual, and practical issues and challenges each of us must face as we grow in our understanding and practice of true worship. That worship of God through his Son Jesus Christ in the sanctifying power of the Holy Spirit embodies the truth, goodness, and beauty of God, inspiring worshippers into God's mission in the world. Dr. Horton writes and lives with a profoundly nurturing heart of an encourager, along with a strong sense of inspiration built on a solid theological foundation. I highly recommend this book."

—*James R. Hart, President*
The Robert E. Webber Institute for Worship Studies

"Windows on Personal Devotion and Prayer" from *Windows on Worship* reminds me of conversations with Wallace Horton when we worked side by side years ago in parish ministry. He reminds us that when worship leaders experience Jesus working in their personal lives through his Word every day of the week, they expect him to be in the house on Sunday morning, too. That's how a leader's quiet time with the Lord can change the culture of a church. Dr. Horton has given us a tool needed for our spiritual tool boxes."

—*John R. Denninger, Bishop/District President*
Southeastern District, Lutheran Church-Missouri Synod

"*Windows on Worship* collects the lifetime reflections of a thoughtful worship minister—a planner, teacher, leader, and fellow worshipper. Each of these small essays is like a drop of dew, long and quietly condensed, able to clear the worship air and water the worshipper's heart."

—*Carla Waterman, Founding Professor*
The Robert E. Webber Institute for Worship Studies

"*Windows on Worship* should be titled *Wisdom on Worship*. In an age when worship has been both rediscovered and cheapened at the same time, this book brings us an encounter with an authentic man of God who knows what it means to worship the living God with head, heart, and hands, and how to lead others as well."

—*John Yates II, Rector Emeritus*
The Falls Church (Anglican), Falls Church, Va.

Windows on Worship

52 Devotional Readings for Those Who Lead, Plan, and Engage in Worshiping God

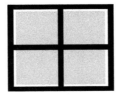

Wallace W. Horton

Foreword by Daniel Sharp

© 2021
Published in the United States by Nurturing Faith, Macon, GA.
Nurturing Faith is a book imprint of Good Faith Media (goodfaithmedia.org).
Library of Congress Cataloging-in-Publication Data is available.

ISBN: 978-1-63528-153-8

All rights reserved. Printed in the United States of America.

All scripture citations are from the NEW AMERICAN STANDARD BIBLE®,
© 1960, 1962, 1963, 1968, 1971, 1972, 1973, 1975, 1977, 1995 by
The Lockman Foundation. Used by permission. https://www.lockman.org/.

Webber Institute Books

Webber Institute Books (WIB) serves as the publishing arm of the Robert E. Webber Institute for Worship Studies (IWS). The Institute was founded by the late Robert E. Webber for the purpose of forming servant leaders in worship renewal with the perspective that "the way to the future necessarily runs through the past." IWS is the only school in North America dedicated solely to graduate education in biblical foundations, historical development, theological reflection, and cultural analysis of worship. Its vision emphasizes that its graduates will "participate intentionally in the story of the Triune God" to "bring renewal in the local and global church by shaping life and ministry according to that story." In scope it is "gospel-centered in nature and ecumenical in outlook, embracing and serving the whole church in its many expressions and variations." Those interested in obtaining further information concerning the Institute should consult www.iws.edu.

Webber Institute Books are published by agreement with Good Faith Media (www.goodfaithmedia.org) to provide a means for disseminating to the general public varying and differing views concerning the many aspects of worship and Christian life. The ideas expressed in these published materials wholly remain the views of the authors themselves and are not necessarily those of IWS or the publisher.

It is the prayerful concern of both IWS and WIB that the information contained in these works will stimulate further reflection and discussion. The results of such exchange of ideas hopefully will enhance worship renewal within the various segments of the Christian church. Moreover, in keeping with the hopes and dreams of Bob Webber, may all that is done through this publishing enterprise enable Christians to reject the narcissistic patterns prevalent in contemporary society and give the glory to God who sent Jesus, the Christ, to provide for human transformation and in concert provided humans with the divine triune presence through the Holy Spirit.

Robert Myers   James Hart
General Editor   President

Gerald L. Borchert
Founding Editor

Dedication

It is with deep affection and love that I dedicate this book to
Dr. William Lock, professor emeritus at Biola University,
who has taught me, guided me, loved me, and shown me what it means
to be a man who loves Jesus and is a true worshiper of God.

Contents

Foreword

Wally Horton has given all of those involved in the worship of the Triune God—Father, Son, and Holy Spirit—a most practical and thought-stimulating gift. Be it pastor, worship leader, musician, worship committee, or lay person, there are many valuable insights into humankind's most significant engagement on earth, the worship of God.

Reading *Windows on Worship* is very much like sitting down and having a one-on-one conversation with a seasoned master. In casual but substantial writing, Dr. Horton shares in a devotional manner, spiritual insights borne of many years of personal experience as to the nature of worship in congregational settings. There is no sugarcoating in his words: he's a realist. Most of us worship leaders have had people come up to us after a worship service with "suggestions" as to where we can improve the service. In this book you will find wise advice: the author does not shy away from discussing difficult moments that occur from time to time as we are involved in worship.

In the 52 insightful essays covering five areas—personal devotion, worship theology and practice, preparing for worship, the church year and worship, and worship that transforms lives—we see the depth of Dr. Horton's heart, his great love for the church, and his passion for worship. This combination makes for compelling reading. The book could be an excellent resource for a weekly study for a team of musicians, a choir, a worship committee, or source of topics for a pastoral staff discussion.

As a teaching church musician his whole life, Dr. Horton challenges those in worship leadership and everyone else to take those hours of corporate worship seriously, offering our very best. Rather than simply making a statement and moving on, he shares the importance of examining our worship perspective. For example, Horton addresses the significance of having children in adult worship or looking at funerals through the eyes of worship. He offers us a challenge to think the bigger picture of worship rather than repeatedly settling for the week-to-week planning. Whether you minister in a contemporary or praise band situation, or a liturgical worship setting, or places in between, you will find valuable insights and thought-provoking ideas from one who has served in all of those situations.

—*Daniel Sharp, DMA*
Professor, The Robert E. Webber Institute for Worship Studies

Acknowledgments

A ministry of 50 years does not occur unless there are hundreds of individuals who support, encourage, and pray during the course of those five decades.

God has richly blessed me with my family, colleagues, friends, and congregational members who have guided me, loved me, and participated with me in various ministry settings and circumstances. It is partially because of these blessings that I have been able to reflect upon and write about areas of worship that are so important to me.

I am thankful to God for the congregations of believers at Bethany Lutheran Church, The Falls Church (Anglican), Prince of Peace Lutheran Church, and Living Savior Lutheran Church. The men and women, and girls and boys, in those settings have been an inspiration to me and a joy to lead and guide in the worship of God. The senior pastors of those congregations—the late Nathan Loesch, John Yates, John Denninger, Ralph Wiechmann, Pete Alexander, and Andy Lissy—have encouraged me and been true colleagues and partners in our shared ministries of worship. I have learned so much from them. The trust and confidence they have placed in me through the years has been one of God's many blessings to me.

Compiling essays, articles, devotional thoughts, and other writings from a ministry that began in 1970 and shaping those works into a collection that is helpful to worship leaders, planners, and participants in the 21st century does not occur in isolation.

I am very grateful to Bob Myers who has served as my general editor throughout the entire process of producing *Windows on Worship*. Without his guidance and encouragement, this project would not have taken place. I am very appreciative of Jim Hart, Dan Sharp, and the entire editorial committee of Webber Institute Books for their encouragement, perspective, and guidance.

Editing, proofreading, and approaching a topic from more than one direction has always been a challenge for me. Every writer needs a special person who can fill this role and provide proper assistance without compromising the overall vision of the writings. Meghan Benson has been that person—a blessing beyond words.

Finally, no person navigates through a half-century of ministry without the love and support of their family. My dear wife Joan has loved me; provided wisdom, insight, comfort, and guidance; and been at my side throughout our life together. Her witness and love for Jesus is an inspiration to me, our children and their spouses, our grandchildren, and all who know her. Joan is a treasure for whom I thank God every day.

Introduction

Those persons who have devoted their lives to something they are passionate about generally have quite a bit to say about the topic. As one who has spent the past 50 years devoting myself to a ministry of planning, shaping, and leading Christian worship, I can certainly identify with that!

Of those 50 years, I spent 45 in full-time ministry at a large Southern California Lutheran congregation, an influential Episcopal/Anglican congregation in Northern Virginia, and a large Lutheran congregation in Northern Virginia. I have had the privilege of serving as a Bible study leader, classroom teacher, minister of worship and music, organist, and occasional preacher. Although I retired from full-time ministry in 2015, I continue to plan worship and serve as a musician on a part-time basis for a modest-size Lutheran congregation in Northern Virginia.

I am not the person I was when my ministry began 50 years ago! The opportunities and experiences that God has afforded me throughout the years have shaped my theology, my worship practices, my understanding of worship, and most importantly, have deepened my walk with the Lord. God's shaping hand has given me opportunities to serve and contribute to my congregations and the greater church in ways I pray have been positive and helpful.

From 1995 to 2015, I was asked to share my thoughts on worship in a series of articles and essays titled "Window on Worship" for *The Journal*, the official periodical of the National Association of Church Musicians (NACM, now disbanded), an organization comprised of representatives of many denominations who served in the areas of worship and choral music and in other areas of ministry in the church. Membership ranged from full-time ministers to those who worked as part-time worship leaders and musicians. The essays written for NACM were designed to help those serving throughout the church who had a wide variety of experience and theological and musical training.

In addition to sharing my thoughts with the NACM membership, I have also had the opportunity to provide devotional writings and meditations for the congregations in which I have served and continue to serve. In both settings, I wrote from a perspective of sharing my personal thoughts and reflections with a varied audience of clergy, church professionals, musicians, and lay people who all shared a love of Christian worship.

My life has been influenced and blessed by Robert Webber, William Lock, Paul Manz, Wilbur Held, and others. In thinking about these personal "giants" in my life, I have recalled that so much of what they shared and taught me came when they were in their late 60s and 70s.

Now that I am well into my 70s, I find myself reflecting on how the Lord has led, allowed, equipped, and taught me over a lifetime in ministry. It is my desire to share some of those reflections and thoughts with you—my friends and colleagues, known and unknown—who are in one way or another a part of the glorious actions and ministry of Christian worship. Whether you are a pastor, a minister of worship and music, a choir member, a praise team member, a lay person in the pew, or serve in some other capacity, you will find devotional thoughts and suggestions that address a variety of topics related to worshiping God—Father, Son, and Holy Spirit.

I wrote each of the "windows on worship" in this book with one of the following objectives:

• to help you strengthen your personal devotional life
• to provide greater awareness of a biblical theology of worship
• to better prepare yourself as you come to worship
• to develop a deeper appreciation for the church year
• to help you recognize how our Triune God transforms lives through worship

Although the essays in this book could be read in one or two sittings, it is my hope that you will read and meditate on one essay per week. Each one includes a passage taken from *The New American Standard Bible* that is intended to serve not only as the basis for each reading, but also as a springboard that may assist you in considering and applying what is shared to your own life. I encourage you to meditate on each Scripture passage prior to reading its corresponding essay. Let the Lord help you focus on what he may want to say to you. Over the course of a single year, you will have completed a journey that will allow you to "connect some of the dots" in your own personal devotion to, application of, and participation in Christian worship.

I offer this book to you as one who has received the benefits and blessings of a lifetime of learning and leading and of planning and sharing worship with God's people. Perhaps not all of the essays and thoughts shared in this book will specifically apply to you in your current ministry, congregational setting, or personal situation. Yet it is my hope and prayer that as you who read this book and use it as a part of your daily walk with Jesus, you will be stretched, encouraged, inspired, and strengthened as you discover fresh and new ways to honor our God—Father, Son, and Holy Spirit—in your worship.

May the Lord open the many "windows on worship" he desires to show you as you read this book.

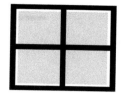

Windows on Personal Devotion and Prayer

What comes to your mind when you think about personal devotion and prayer? Is it sitting down with a cup of coffee and reading from Oswald Chambers' *My Utmost for His Highest*? Perhaps it is a prayer from John Baille's *A Diary of Private Prayer*. It could simply be closing your eyes and thinking about God's holiness or praying the Lord's Prayer. Maybe you take time each morning to focus on what lies before you while asking for God's blessing as you commit your day to him.

There are likely as many answers to my initial question as there are individuals who might answer it. Each of the suggested answers can be wonderful spiritual disciplines. Often, though, it is possible to succumb to the danger of routineness or "business as usual," especially if you are involved in full-time ministry or very active as a lay person in your church. We can fall into a spiritual trap of focusing more on the format of the action than the content of the discipline.

All of us face obstacles that have the potential to distract us from focusing our hearts and minds on Jesus and his love for us. Those who aspire to lead God's people in worship need to be encouraged to commit themselves to times of personal devotion and prayer. This is a lifelong challenge for all who desire to follow the Good Shepherd.

The essays found in this section are offered as suggestions to help you explore ways to strengthen your prayer life, your personal and corporate worship, and those times of solitude in your private devotions.

Each of the nine windows that follow provide thoughts intended to help you in this endeavor of deepening your walk with the Lord. Whether through the use of "listening prayer," personal quiet times, or one of the other means addressed, it is my prayer that you will discover a thought or suggestion in these devotionals that will assist you in your spiritual growth.

God bless you as you draw closer to the Lord through personal devotion and prayer.

Private, Personal, and Public

Come, let us worship and bow down.
(Ps. 95:6a)

During my time as a student at the Robert E. Webber Institute for Worship Studies, I formed many wonderful relationships and received life-changing instruction. I clearly remember one of our class sessions when we were discussing our congregations and worship settings. Although we came from different denominations, it was interesting to hear how much our churches had in common, especially when we thought about the people rather than the organizational labels. We were reminded of the similarities of people, regardless of the worship styles. My class members also noted how alike individuals were when it comes to expressing their faith publicly.

It was then that one of our professors reminded us that while our <u>faith may be personal, it is never private.</u> I thought about that statement for a long time and how it applies to worship. There is such a thing as private worship. Hopefully all of us set apart some moments each day to be alone with the Lord. In the truest sense, though, our corporate worship as the body of Christ is not private. It is always public and hopefully always personal. Our worship is visible for everyone in the world to witness. It is a witness to the world of who and whose we are. It is the testimony of a beacon in a dark world that says, "Jesus is Lord" (1 Cor. 12:3). We must not forget this truth.

Our worship must also be personal. I am not suggesting that corporate worship will be exactly the way we want it to be. Many of us may have dealt with individuals who have made the statement, "I didn't like this or that about the worship service this morning." I remember a story told by a well-known worship leader at a conference a number of years ago. A lady came up to the choir director following a service and said, "I didn't like the anthem this morning." The choir director politely received her comment and smiled. He affirmed her right to her personal feelings and at the same time kindly shared that some things in worship are meant to be God-centered rather than people-centered. He made the point that not everything in worship is intended to please all of the people all of the time. Rather, it is through worship where we give our praise to God. As we direct our worship to God, he comes to us and speaks to us. In and through the actions and symbols of worship, all of us have the opportunity for a personal encounter with the living Lord. As we participate in the various expressions of the Eucharist and the Word, we can and do meet Jesus in the most intimate of ways.

Corporate worship should be both personal *and* public. Worship is where we tell and enact God's story together. It is where we witness to the world and where God meets us and fills the needs we have in our spiritual, emotional, and physical lives. What wonderful gifts we receive from our God!

Listening: The Gift of Prayer

Cease striving and know that I am God.
(Ps. 46:10a)

Prayer is one of the great gifts from our Lord. There are numerous examples throughout Scripture that demonstrate the power of prayer: from prophets praying, to King David and others praying the psalms, to disciples asking Jesus about prayer, to St. Paul teaching about prayer, to times when our Lord went off by himself to pray. Prayer is, indeed, a gift that we must not neglect in our personal devotion time.

Prayer also plays an important part in our time together as the worshiping body of Christ. An opening prayer for worship, the Prayer of the Day, the Lord's Prayer, prayer before and after Communion, and the prayers of the people are examples of the use of prayer in in our corporate worship.

However, one of the areas that you may not have considered both in your personal and corporate worship is "listening prayer," those times when you follow the direction of the psalmist to "cease striving and know that I am God" (Ps. 46:10). I love the words of the *King James Version* where the writer directs us to "be still."

I am reminded of a story I heard the Christian sociologist, Tony Campolo, tell once. During an interview, Mother Teresa was asked, "When you pray to God, what do you say?" Mother Teresa replied, "I don't say anything; I listen." The interviewer, a bit puzzled, continued by asking, "Alright, when you pray, what does God say to you?" Mother Teresa replied, "God doesn't say anything; God listens."[1] Mother Teresa's point was that God is not limited to speaking to us audibly. He often "speaks" to us in silence much as he spoke to Elijah in the "sound of a gentle blowing" (1 Kgs. 19:12). Many [ti]mes we need to be listening in our stillness to hear God's voice.

There are times in our prayer life when we are so occupied telling God what we [need] and want that we fail to listen. It may take a little time to "hear from God," but as [Oswa]ld Chambers reminds us, "Time is nothing to God."[2] "God is never in a hurry."[3] [Sometime]s God speaks with us through silence as we wait. The historic practice of *Lectio* [Divina i]s a powerful means to use as we read Scripture, meditate, pray, and listen for [God's voi]ce.

[There are sacr]ed times in our private and corporate prayer when we simply listen. God hears [our moments o]f silence. May we hear God's silence as God speaks to us in the stillness of [these sacred mo]ments.

Personal Times with a Personal God

In the morning, O LORD, You will hear my voice;
In the morning I will order my prayer to You and eagerly watch.
(Ps. 5:3)

During my years in ministry, I have considered more than once the difficulty of being an active worshiper while leading corporate worship. It is not easy to be personally focused while leading and helping others.

Individual worship is a different matter. Those who plan and lead congregational worship need to make a commitment and take the time to have a personal time of daily worship. As a plant withers without water and nourishment, the same is true for worship leaders. It is true that God inhabits the praises of his people, but it is equally true that the Lord wants to hear from us on an individual basis and for us to hear from him.

Leadership requires great energy and focus. Often, leaders do not have the opportunity to be as fully engaged in giving themselves in corporate worship as someone sitting in the pew. Worship leaders need to have daily spiritual "refills and tune-ups" that keep them in touch with God. Those times of quiet and personal devotion may take on a variety of forms. There are numerous writings, prayers, and meditations that can help inspire and guide individuals in daily meetings with the Lord. Denominational devotionals also are available. Some of the classic works of writers such as Oswald Chambers, Henri Nouwen, or John Baille can also lead us through a time of personal worship.

Do not leave personal worship time to chance. Establish a time that will be prioritized and works for you. Time that is not intentionally set aside for this purpose will soon get lost in the busyness of your day. For many people, early morning works best. Regardless of the time you choose, I urge you to commit yourself to the practice of individual worship. By meeting God early in the day, you will be in agreement with the hymn writer, Thomas Ken (1637–1711), who wrote the following verses:

Awake, my soul, and with the sun Thy daily stage of duty run;
Shake off dull sloth and joyful rise to pay thy morning sacrifice.

Lord, I my vows to Thee renew; disperse my sins as morning dew;
Guard my first springs of thought and will and with Thyself my spirit fill.

Direct, control, suggest this day all I design or do or say
That all my pow'rs with all their might in Thy sole glory may unite.

Praise God, from whom all blessings flow; Praise Him all creatures here below;
Praise Him above, ye heavenly host: Praise Father, Son, and Holy Ghost.[4]

Finding Time to Worship

Ascribe to the LORD the glory due His name;
Bring an offering, and come before Him;
Worship the LORD in holy array.
(1 Chron. 16:29)

"When do you get to worship?" That question has been asked of me a number of times. Perhaps it sounds somewhat curious. However, if you think about it, you soon realize that it is a valid question for those who are in worship leadership positions.

Whether you are in the chancel, on the platform, behind the altar, in the pulpit, on the organ bench, or on the podium in front of the choir or orchestra, there are certain responsibilities and duties that require you to be in a different role than those in the congregation. Those who lead need to think and plan ahead to help others in their worship. This is not to say that you cannot derive many of the same benefits as the worshiping congregation. However, those of us who serve as leaders in worship may offer our worship differently in a corporate setting than others. By the outpouring of ourselves in leading and serving others, we are offering our worship and praise to God.

How do you find time to worship without the "distractions" of being a worship leader? One way is to meditate on and pray over those elements for which you have direct responsibility prior to the service. If you are directing a choir and those duties include a call to worship, a psalm, and an anthem, pray with your choir about those musical selections at your rehearsal.

If you are playing the organ or the piano for the service, read through the texts of the hymns and choruses. You may discover ways to improvise on a text that will help your people derive a clearer meaning of what the writer is saying. At the same time, it may give you an opportunity to hear God speak through the text in a new way.

Make a determined effort to listen to and apply those things in worship for which you are not directly responsible. For example, if you are the musician, give an extra measure of your attention to the reading of Scripture and the sermon. If you are the pastor, listen more carefully to the texts of the anthems and hymns.

Your own time of personal worship and devotion in addition to these practices of prayer, study, and listening during and outside of corporate worship will empower you in ministry and deepen your walk with the Lord.

Soli Deo Gloria

... whatever you do, do all to the glory of God.
(1 Cor. 10:31)

If not the greatest composer who ever lived, Johann Sebastian Bach is certainly near the top of the list. The works produced by this 18th century German Lutheran are unparalleled. His instrumental, keyboard, and vocal music continues to be played and sung throughout the world in a variety of settings, including thousands of churches.

I remember with great fondness a conversation I had many years ago with the late organist Paul Manz. I said to him, "Dr. Manz, if someone was going to take all of my organ music from me and would only let me keep one composer, I would keep your compositions." With a twinkle in his eye, Dr. Manz looked at me and said, "Wally, what would you do with Bach?" That question back to me demonstrated the reverence Dr. Manz had for Bach and his lifetime of work.

Bach never differentiated between secular and sacred music. He wrote everything to the glory of God. His work was an outpouring of his life. Bach had the regular practice of inscribing the letters "SDG" at the conclusion of each of his compositions. Those letters were a reference to the Latin phrase *Soli Deo Gloria* . . . "To God Alone Be the Glory." Bach lived and carried out his work solely for God's glory. He expressed his theology through his music, and displayed that theology for all to hear and appreciate. Bach did not compromise in what he offered for God's glory.

Bach's example is a powerful lesson for all of us to witness and model. By being mindful of committing our daily tasks and work to God's glory we have an opportunity to demonstrate to the world our desire to honor God in all we do.

Bach faced challenges in his life including the deaths of 10 of his 20 children during their childhood. He had his "ups and downs." We do too. However, like Bach, even in our "ups and downs," we can be certain that God will continue to empower and equip us to do our best in response to what God has done for us through Jesus.

God provides for us and will continue to do so. Because of God's assurance, we can with confident hearts inscribe the letters *SDG* on every day of our life.

May God bless you as you dedicate each day to God's glory.

Walking in the Light, Walking as a Child

But if we walk in the Light as He Himself is in the Light, we have fellowship
with one another, and the blood of Jesus His Son cleanses us from all sin.
(1 John 1:7)

One of my favorite hymns is "I Want to Walk as a Child of the Light." The text and tune were written by Kathleen Thomerson (b. 1934) in 1966. I first became familiar with this hymn in 1989. While it is included in the Epiphany section of some hymnals, its message is appropriate at any time during the church year.

The flowing and melodious tune could stand by itself. It truly is a beautiful melody. However, when the text is wedded with the tune, a powerful "musical sermon" is created for each of us to meditate upon and celebrate.

When we sing this hymn during worship at my church, I am reminded of several biblical texts. In Matthew 18:3, Jesus says, "unless you are converted and become like children, you will not enter the kingdom of heaven." There is something about a child-like faith that removes any doubts we might possess. In 1 John 1:7 we read, "but if we walk in the Light … the blood of Jesus His Son cleanses us from all sin." Light, especially the Light of Jesus, has a way of giving each of us direction for focusing on things of an eternal nature.

The hymn by Thomerson not only speaks of us walking in the Light, but also gives us the opportunity to sing of our willingness "to see the brightness of God," "to follow Jesus," "to look at Jesus," and "to be with Jesus." The reason we should desire all of those things is summarized in the words, "In him there is no darkness at all." Jesus gives us a Light that never goes out. His Light is never eclipsed in our souls. There may be times when our own nature tries to keep us in the darkness, yet the Light of Jesus never fails. It always outshines the darkness. It is Jesus' nature and desire to shine in and through us each day of our life.

As you sing this wonderful hymn, not only in Epiphany but throughout the year, keep the prayer, "Shine in my heart, Lord Jesus," on your lips and in your heart.

God bless you as you walk as a child in the Light of Jesus.

Finding a Place to Pray

After He had sent the crowds away, He went up on the mountain by Himself to pray:
and when it was evening, He was there alone.
(Matt. 14:23)

Jesus sought time alone to pray. For him, he found comfort being in the mountains. Matthew 14:23, Mark 4:64, Luke 6:12, and John 6:15 all share different accounts of Jesus praying. The connecting thread in these references from the Gospels is that even in the midst of his various ministries and miracles, Jesus took the time to retreat to the mountains and be alone and pray to his Father.

Retreating is finding that little secluded area where you can be alone for reflection and meditation. One of my dear friends and mentors shared a story with me years ago when we were on a retreat in the mountains with several other music ministers. He had risen very early. In those first hours of the day, he found his quiet place of seclusion. It was there that the Lord shared with him how my family and I would be moving from a West Coast ministry setting to a new ministry in Virginia. This message became a reality several months later. The stillness of his quiet place provided a setting where the Lord chose to speak to my friend in a very unique and direct way.

How many of us have gone to our places of solitude, our "prayer closets," by ourselves and spent an evening praying? There is something about praying during the night hours that can touch our souls and strengthen our spirits in a special way. The psalmist tells us, "When I remember You on my bed, I meditate on You in the night watches, for You have been my help, and in the shadow of Your wings I sing for joy" (Ps. 63:6-7).

May we be led to follow the example of Jesus and identify our place of solitude, where we pray, share our heart's desire, sing for joy, and hear our Lord's voice as he speaks to us.

Prayer Changes Things

Return and say to Hezekiah the leader of My people,
"Thus says the LORD, the God of your father David, 'I have heard your prayer,
I have seen your tears; behold, I will heal you.'"
(2 Kgs. 20:5a)

On my desk at home I have a 12"x3" plaque inscribed with the words, "Prayer Changes Things." I first heard this motto many years ago. Occasionally I would listen to a radio ministry that concluded each broadcast with those words. At the time, the words did not have a great impact on my prayer life. However, over the years, that saying has come to mean more and more to me.

Prayer is something we may prefer to keep as a "private matter" or rely upon only when we are facing a situation that appears overwhelming. But prayer is more than a private matter or practice we turn to when circumstances are beyond our control. I would encourage you to rely upon it as a wonderful gift from God that allows you to call upon him for your needs, to give him praise and thanks, and to listen to his voice and will. There are several ways to include these thoughts as you plan congregational worship. I would suggest two.

First, how much time do you spend in prayer prior to those moments when you plan a worship service? How much time do you commit to asking the Lord if there is something he would like you to do or consider as you are preparing? It can be tempting to go from one week to the next with a "business as usual" mentality while planning the services or filling in the blanks of the liturgy. How much time do you listen for what God might want to tell you as you prepare for that weekly event which is the highest priority of the church?

Second, how much do you use corporate and individual prayer in worship services? I am not simply talking about the Collect (Prayer) of the Day or the prepared prayers from the prayer book. I am speaking of opportunities when people can spontaneously pray in periods of silence or have the opportunity to come forward and pray with others.

Since prayer changes things, we have a high calling as leaders to rely upon it as we prepare weekly worship settings for the people we serve in our congregations. At one church where I served, we used to ask, "What is our level of expectation in worship? Do we expect people to leave worship differently than when they arrived?" People are changed through praying and seeing God act.

I pray that you will use prayer as a means of hearing God as you prepare worship and that you will afford your people the opportunity to use personal prayer in their corporate worship. God bless you as you see God change things.

Windows on Worship

The Use of Prayer in Worship

The LORD has heard my supplication,
The LORD receives my prayer.
(Ps. 6:9)

Most Christians understand that prayer is a gift that God has given to the church and its people to communicate and share our deepest needs and desires with him. I cannot think of any Christian worship service I have ever attended where there wasn't at least one prayer included. It might have been a pastoral prayer, a corporate prayer, or the Lord's Prayer. But some sort of prayer was included.

In my tradition, there are normally several prayers included in each service. The Prayer of the Day (which touches upon the liturgical theme for the day), the Prayers of the People of God (which often ends each petition with "Lord in your mercy, hear our prayer"), the Lord's Prayer, and the Post-Communion Prayer are all examples of prayers that are usually part of our worship. We have become accustomed to them. We expect them. For some of us, it would not seem like a worship service without these prayers. However, have they become so commonplace, so ordinary, that we take them for granted and minimize their effectiveness in our lives?

At a church where I served, we introduced the use of prayer partners and prayer stations during worship. We provided individuals the opportunity to meet the Lord in worship through prayer and to experience divine, life-changing power. These opportunities occurred during the time of Holy Communion distribution. As people came forward to receive the bread and the wine, they also had the opportunity to go to a designated area off to the side of the sanctuary where they could request private prayer with a prayer partner. The prayer partner listened to each person's request and then prayed for God's spiritual, physical, and relational healing presence in their life. When we began this practice, some people would come forward for personal prayer every time it was offered during Holy Communion. It was an affirmation to us that there were many in our pews every week who realized that they had areas in their lives that needed God's healing touch through personal prayer.

How much time is devoted to prayer in your services? Does prayer receive the attention it deserves? In a study conducted by Dr. Constance Cherry, her research of 31 worship services over a period of 16 months in 19 different denominational settings revealed that in traditional worship, 13 percent of the worship time was devoted to prayer. In contemporary settings, 5 percent of the worship time was devoted to prayer.[5]

The opportunity for meaningful and personal prayer in worship is an important gift to consider. Worship is a time when we can meet God in the most intimate of ways. Praying with one another about specific and deeply felt needs and concerns is another way to experience God's life-changing presence in worship.

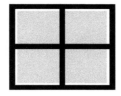

Windows on Reflections of
Worship Theology and Practice

Possessing a theology of worship and having a philosophy of how we practice that theology helps to shape and define who we are as worshipers. For many, fourfold worship (Gathering, Word, Table, and Sending) is the heart of what defines and comprises a worship service that is both historically based and also relevant to the 21st century.

There is likely, however, great diversity among planners, leaders, and participants as to the details and expressions of worship. What should worship look like? Who should be involved in worship? What elements of worship are negotiable (and nonnegotiable)? These are examples of questions that can lead to misunderstandings and disagreements in the local church.

The 11 essays in this section address topics such as: What is worship? What happens in worship? How can I include "new" expressions of worship? How do children learn to worship?

In addition, the essays offer suggestions to help worship leaders and planners carefully think about their own worship theology. By reflecting upon and considering our practices, we have the potential to help all of our worshiping community receive the many benefits and blessings available to us when we encounter our Lord in worship.

May you be encouraged and open to the leading of God's Holy Spirit as you consider these topics.

The Economy of the Trinity in Worship

He saw the heavens opening, and the Spirit like a dove descending upon Him; and a voice came out of the heavens ... "You are My beloved Son, in You I am well-pleased."
(Mark 1:11)

I have been a Lutheran all my life. I was baptized as an infant, confirmed in, and attended eight years of parochial school, all in the Lutheran Church. Even during the 11 years when I served in an Episcopal/Anglican setting, I was still a Lutheran! The rector, the vestry, the congregation, and I all knew it. We were all happy!

From my earliest days until now, I have usually been present in worship services that begin with a Trinitarian invocation: "In the name of the Father, and of the Son, and of the Holy Spirit, Amen." The times of confession and absolution often conclude with the words by the pastor, "I forgive you all of your sins in the name of the Father, and of the Son, and of the Holy Spirit, Amen." Most of the services I have been a part of have concluded with either the Aaronic Blessing from Numbers 6:24-26 or St. Paul's blessing from 2 Corinthians 13:14. These examples provide a foundation for an understanding of the ministry of the Trinity in worship.

The Father's creative and sustaining presence, the Son's redeeming love and resurrection power, and the Holy Spirit's transformational healing and sanctification are available to all who come into God's presence to worship in faith and with expectation. As God's nature is perfect and complete, so is this interacting ministry of the Trinity, where each member has a separate role in our lives and in our worship.

The reality for some worship settings, however, can be an overemphasis of the work and personality of one member of the Trinity at the expense of the other two. Examples of this can be seen in primarily emphasizing the need for spiritual gifts, or focusing mainly on the sovereignty of the Father, or having a "personal relationship" with Jesus to the extent that the community of believers is neglected.

In worship we remember, reenact, and participate in God's story of creation, redemption, and life-changing transformation. Failure to do this results in what Robert Webber calls "the fragmentation of worship."[1] In fragmented worship, worshipers are deprived of the fullness of all that God wants to share with us.

Perhaps you are in a worship setting that places most of its "theological eggs" in one basket and thereby unintentionally fails to receive either a historical or contemporary expression of what the Triune God offers and conveys through Christian worship. I urge you to explore this essential work of the Trinity. You and your congregation will be blessed. As you are led by our wonderful God, I commend to you the final verse of the ninth-century hymn attributed to Rabanus Maurus (776–856), "Come, Holy Ghost, Creator Blest": "Praise we the Father and the Son and Holy Spirit, with them One, and may the Son on us bestow the gifts that from the Spirit flow!"[2]

A Personal Definition of Worship

God is spirit, and those who worship Him
must worship in spirit and truth.
(John 4:24)

One of my fondest memories is the time I spent at Biola University in the mid-1980s pursuing a master's degree in church music. It was during that time the Lord blessed me with guidance from, mentoring by, and a deep friendship with Dr. William Lock. This relationship continues to this day, and for it I am continually thankful to the Lord.

I will never forget the course on worship that I took with Dr. Lock. At the initial meeting of the class, the first thing he asked us to do was to write down our personal definition of Christian worship. I wrote that "Christian worship is our response to God for what he has done for us through his Son, Jesus Christ."

When we talk about worship, we may believe that all of us are talking about the same thing. However, the definitions that were read by the class members that day revealed just the opposite. Many of the outward appearances of worship can be similar in churches. Yet when we ask individuals about their expectations and understanding of what worship is and what it should be, we may find many diverse opinions. Our own understanding of objective theology (God's action) versus subjective theology (our reaction and response) will have a great influence upon our personal definition. This is not a positive or a negative: it is simply a reality.

As you think about your personal definition of Christian worship, it can be helpful to explore what others have expressed:

- William Temple: "To worship is to quicken the conscience by the holiness of God, to feed the mind with the truth of God, to purge the imagination by the beauty of God, to open the heart to the love of God, to devote the will to the purpose of God."[3]
- Evelyn Underhill: "Christian worship is the response of the creature to the Eternal."[4]
- Harold Best: "Worship is an expression of insufficiency."[5]

Whatever you establish as your definition of Christian worship, I encourage you to hold it before yourself as a measuring rod as you prepare, lead, and engage in worship with the body of Christ.

Worship: The Hub of Spiritual Transformation

. . . be transformed by the renewing of your mind . . .
(Rom. 12:2)

Worship leaders, planners, and participants spend a lot of time thinking about what occurs in worship. They have hopes, dreams, and expectations regarding both the content and the end result. Each is hopeful that the pastor will have a strong message, that the choir will sing well, and that there are no surprises that might detract from the carefully planned service. Pastors and musicians will likely feel that it has been a good morning of worship if those things occur and no one comes up after the service to register a complaint or give a negative opinion.

In coming to that conclusion, I am reminded of two songs that were popular in the 1960s and 1970s: "Is That All There Is?" and "What's It All About, Alfie?" If all that we look for in worship is to keep things running smoothly and avoiding negative comments, we are missing the mark.

Several years ago I was asked to speak at a neighboring church on the topic of worship. During the morning break a man came up to me and shared his reasons why he attended church: He wanted to (1) see his friends and (2) to hear a "good sermon." He told me that he usually achieved his first objective, but that he rarely achieved the second. Then he proceeded into an editorial tirade about the sermons of the pastor, who was also present that morning. When an opportune time allowed me to interject a response, I suggested to the man that it would probably be appropriate for him to share his concerns with the pastor. One can imagine where the conversation went from there!

My purpose in mentioning this episode is to highlight the misunderstanding that worship is "about us." Rather, worship is about God. It is also important to keep in mind that through the preaching of the Word, sacraments and ordinances, the sacred actions of worship, and the prayers of the people, God's power is present to change us when we participate in Christian worship regardless of our tradition. Christian worship conveys life-changing power.

At one of the churches where I served, we used the phrase, "Worship is the hub of spiritual transformation." We are reminded in 2 Corinthians 3:18 that when we behold the "glory of the Lord" with an "unveiled face," we are transformed. When we meet Jesus in worship, we are changed. Spiritual transformation can, and does, take place in worship when we meet God in a personal and powerful way.

Do you expect to be different when you leave worship than when you arrived? Expectation is an important part of worship. When we expect to meet God in worship, we can be, and are, changed. God's life-changing power is present and waiting to meet us.

God bless you in your worship!

The Cultural Accommodation of Christian Worship

And do not be conformed to this world . . .
(Rom. 12:2)

We hear and read a lot about various worship styles and practices. There will always be different opinions regarding these topics this side of heaven. One question, though, can be addressed that applies to every expression and practice: "How do we approach worship?"

The culture of the 21st century has created a climate that allows for attitudes of casualness, informality, and giving less than our best effort. There are some venues where mediocrity is an accepted standard and the expected norm. Excellence and attention to detail are no longer required in many settings. The attitude of "doing just enough to get by" has become standard operating procedure. If you don't believe that, simply think back over some of the experiences you might have had recently at a retail department store, a hardware store, or a fast-food outlet. Think of some of the frustrations you might have realized when trying to get technical support or an answer to what seemingly was a fairly simple question. When is the last time a school district raised the standards for students to receive a letter grade of "A"? The point in all of these examples is to demonstrate how the bar has been lowered in many areas of life. Consider how this lowering of standards relates to worship:

- What are the expectations of ourselves, our colleagues, our choir members, our praise team members, our orchestra members, and the other individuals with whom we minister?
- Have we allowed our worldly culture to determine what represents the best we can offer in our various worship styles?
- What are the expectations we hold up for our congregation members as they come to worship?
- What is the standard for encouraging people to be regular in their worship attendance?
- Is worship a priority, or is it simply an option among many choices?
- As we prepare and plan our worship services each week, are we committed to the highest standard possible in our traditions or are we satisfied with less than our best effort?

I love Anne Ortlund's thoughts from her book, *Up with Worship*: "Weekly worship is the highest corporate act of the body of Christ. It is the visible demonstration that he is 'Priority One' to us and our church. We must pray over it, labor over it, and shape it."[6] She's got it right. Worship deserves our best!

I encourage you to avoid the temptation of a casual culture. Do not allow your worship to be influenced by an attitude of mediocrity and cutting corners. Keep striving for the best. Remember to whom our worship is directed. That should provide each of us with a powerful incentive to make our worship experience the very best it can be.

Remembering as Part of Our Worship

Lord, You have been our dwelling place in all generations.
(Ps. 90:1)

To remember, to recall: This is what we do in our worship services when we take the time to reflect upon all that God has done for us in Jesus Christ. We recall God's faithful deeds for us. We remember what God has done for each of us personally. Obviously, these remembrances will take on different perspectives for each of us. When we sing, "O God, Our Help in Ages Past," we will be affected differently. None of us has had the exact same life experience—similar, perhaps; identical, very unlikely.

We can be certain, however, that in each of our own worship experiences and traditions, there are opportunities to remember and express our gratitude and thanks for what God has done for us. We can do this through hymns, choruses, prayers, the Communion liturgy, and even our stewardship of time, treasure, and talent.

As important as it is for us to remember, even more important is the fact that God remembers! In the Lutheran tradition there is a post-communion canticle that reminds us that, "He recalls His promises and leads His people forth in joy."[7] Aren't you glad that God remembers? Aren't you glad that God is not like us and becomes forgetful? Aren't you glad that God leads forth in joy?

While remembering what God has done for us, it is just as important to claim God's promises and be aware of all that he continues to do for us. As a wise friend once shared, "Worship is more about God than it is about us." Worship is that time when we gather as the people of God and actively remember, recall, and celebrate what God has done, is doing, and will continue to do. These actions of recalling to mind and reenacting God's story (anamnesis) are most obvious when we gather at the Table to receive the gifts of bread and wine.

Regardless of your theological perspective and understanding of the Lord's Supper, all who participate in this action are doing what our Lord commands in Luke 22:19. We are remembering. We are reenacting and participating in God's story. We are celebrating the great reality that "Christ has died! Christ is risen! Christ will come again!" By acknowledging and believing this truth, we receive our Lord's promise of resurrection power in our lives.

As worshipers, may we all remember that God is faithful. May each of us possess the peace that passes all understanding, trusting that God always keeps his promises. God never forgets us. God always remembers that we are his children.

All of this is worth remembering. Thank you, God.

How Do You Spell "Us"?

And the congregation of those who believed were of one heart and soul.
(Acts 4:32a)

I have had the privilege of speaking to groups of ministers throughout my years in ministry. On one occasion, I was talking with 20 Lutheran pastors from my geographical area. The topic was "Lutheran Worship: Where we have been, where we are at, and where we are going." This group of pastors represented different perspectives, ideas, and experiences. While preparing my comments, I anticipated that there could be some disagreement in the group over a few thoughts I would be sharing. Acknowledging that reality was a freeing experience for me. I went into the presentation with my eyes wide open, understanding that I was not going to have total and complete agreement from everyone who would be present.

After discussing the "Where we have been" and "Where we are at" material, we moved into "Where we are going." I was pleased to observe that there was a significant amount of common understanding and agreement from the group. Everyone agreed that it was essential to be faithful to the doctrines regarding the Word and the sacraments. At the same time, there was an awareness and acknowledgement that there needed to be an openness to new forms and expressions of worship that had not been a part of the past.

One of the challenges of moving into new expressions and forms of worship is dealing with a cultural and consumer mentality that places a high emphasis on individuals and their preferences, rather than focusing on the body of Christ. Many congregations have dealt with that situation in recent years. Each of us could likely share stories of individuals in our churches who believe that worship is about them and how they feel.

Weekly corporate worship is an expression of the community of faith that is God-centered. It is about "us," not "I." One of my avocations that used to offer a diversion from my ministry at church was coaching high school girls' basketball. It was a wonderful experience. I loved it! I would talk to my team at the beginning of each season about our goals and expectations. Each year I reminded the girls that there is no "I" in "team." The same is true of corporate worship.

For some people, the concept of "us" rather than "I" can be a challenge. Some are reluctant to give up personal preferences. They do not want to try anything new or different. It is important to be aware of those feelings and in those situations offer a pastoral and caring response to those individuals that can lead to a new trust and love for everyone involved.

Moving into the Future While Connecting with the Past

Behold, I will do something new …
Will you not be aware of it?
(Isa. 43:19a)

We observe All Saints' Day at my church. It is a day that always has great significance for us, one of celebration and great emotion. It is a day when we give thanks for the past and also anticipate the future. This is the time when we remember all of those family members and friends who have died in the past year. We mention each person by name. We pray a prayer of thanksgiving for their lives among us, and we take time to reflect upon the fact that at some time in the future, each of us will be part of an All Saints' Day remembrance. Even as we think about and remember the past, we are preparing for the future.

Our worship life and practices are an extension of what occurs on All Saints' Day. Hopefully, each one of us takes the time to occasionally reflect upon past worship experiences and thank the Lord for those times. While those experiences may not be part of our current practices, they have played an important role in shaping our thoughts and reflections about our worship. We glean from those past times concepts and beliefs that help bring us to where we are now. As we have been shaped and influenced by those who have gone before us, so our thoughts and preferences are partially shaped by our past experiences. However, we are not limited by our past any more than we are an exact copy of someone who has had a role in shaping and influencing us.

As we move on from the present and look forward to new occurrences in our lives, we remain open to the leading of the Spirit to show us new and creative ways to worship God and to help our congregations worship him. If we only stayed "in the past," or at best "in the moment," during our celebration of All Saints' Day, we would never realize the full potential that God has given each of us. In the same way, if we never move beyond the past or what we currently practice, we would be neglecting God's invitation to exercise his gifts to us of creativity and fresh thoughts.

On one occasion, a gentleman in one of the classes I was teaching on worship asked, "Why do we need to be changing things all the time?" I responded that the church and its worship is similar to a seed that one plants in the ground. It is never dormant: it is either growing or dying, dependent upon the nourishment it receives. Our worship can be the same way. Even in traditions and worship forms that have been practiced for centuries, our worship is never dormant. It is energized by the power of the Holy Spirit. It is, in fact, alive and growing!

As you think about and plan worship experiences for your congregations, may you do so with a sincere thankfulness for the past, an appreciation of the present, and an eager anticipation of what God will show you for the future.

Taking a Chance with Worship

Behold, God is my salvation, I will trust and not be afraid;
For the LORD GOD is my strength and song,
And He has become my salvation.
(Isa. 12:2)

Have you ever "taken a chance" with worship? Have you ever been intentional about exploring and experiencing styles of Christian worship that are different from what is normally practiced in your denomination? Has there ever been a time when you took a "leap of faith" outside of your comfort zone to observe how other Christians worship the Lord?

Have you had the experience of someone in your church coming to you after worship and voicing their displeasure about an element in the service? Perhaps it was about a song or anthem, or a prayer, or a liturgical dance. Many times these criticisms are simply given because an individual has never been in a setting that differs from what they normally experience. Objectivity is usually not part of the opinion being expressed.

The longer I have served in church ministry and worship leadership, the more convinced I have become of how many individuals never give themselves permission or allow themselves to experience a "new" style of or form of worship from what they are most familiar. This can be as simple as a newer translation of a hymn text, people raising their hands, praise bands leading a hymn, or worship leaders chanting the liturgy. Many churches have those individuals who are not willing to "take a chance" with worship. Taking a chance requires change. Change is not new to the church: It has been present throughout history, from accepting Gentiles into the church in Acts 15, to new hymnals and prayer books being introduced in denominations.

I urge you to identify an element in your worship service that allows for variation and then present it in a manner that differs from how it is normally presented. Help your people grow in their understanding of the fact that there are many ways to worship God that are pleasing to him. Educate and teach them. Be willing to "take a chance" so that those you serve might experience a fuller understanding and appreciation of how the larger body of Christ worships and acknowledges the king of the universe.

Taking a chance is worth the effort. Not only will it help your congregation grow, but it will also help you grow in your high calling of being a worship leader. William Lock has taught me many things about worship. One of the reasons he was able to do that is because he has always been willing to take a chance with worship. He has served in many different denominations and has used those experiences to help others, like myself, understand the importance of continuing to grow and being stretched. May I encourage you to stretch your people and yourself as you continue to serve the Lord.

Making Time for Worship

For a thousand years in Your sight
Are like yesterday when it passes by,
Or as a watch in the night.
(Ps. 90:4)

I remember the time my wife and I sent our 18-year-old son off to college for the first time. We had a lot of mixed emotions. If you have had children leave home, you know what I mean. I kept thinking, "Where has the time gone?" It seemed that only yesterday we brought our baby boy home from the hospital. Then in the blink of an eye, he was in college. Those years passed quickly.

All of us are aware of time. We are all governed by it in our lives. When someone says, "I don't have time," what they are really saying is, "I choose to use my time in another way." Each of us has the same 24 hours in a day. It simply comes down to how we use it.

Have you ever thought about how we allow time to govern us as we experience worship? In some traditions, any service longer than an hour is unheard of. After an hour, some individuals begin to squirm. Others start looking at their watch. Some simply leave the service. There are those whose idea of a "good" worship service is a "short" worship service. In some instances, quality and content are sacrificed for adhering to a mentality of sticking to a strict timeframe at any cost. That is unfortunate. I wonder if this approach to worship leaves any room for the possibility of Spirit-led spontaneity in a service.

To be clear, a service lasting 90 minutes does not guarantee that it will be more meaningful than a service lasting 60 minutes. There are times when it is appropriate to plan a service that adheres to a structured timeframe. Some occasions require services to be designed for those where the attention span is not as great as it might be for others.

Shortly after we moved to the East Coast, my wife told me that she had stopped wearing a watch to church. When I asked her why, she said that the services progressed in such a way that the time always seemed to move more quickly than she thought it would. Before she knew it, the service was over and it was an hour and a half later! Her response brought to my mind the old Finnish proverb, "God didn't create hurry."

If you think about what Scripture tells us regarding worship in heaven, you can be certain that no one is or will be looking at their watch! As a matter of fact, no one will ever need to ask the question, "Where has the time gone?"

How Do You Teach Children to Worship?

... Permit the children to come to Me; do not hinder them ...
(Mark 10:14)

The six years I spent teaching choral music to seventh- and eighth-grade students at our local middle school has been one of the great joys in my life. We sang every day and talked about different facets of the choral art. Small groups demonstrated and sang for the rest of the class. We sang concerts throughout the year. The students were introduced to music that was out of their reach when they began, but eventually was within their ability to perform. These children learned by listening, observing, asking, and doing.

It has been my experience that most children enjoy learning and being taught. They may not know how to sing. They may feel embarrassed. However, they will respond in positive ways if they are provided with the tools and shown the enjoyment of singing.

Teaching children to worship is similar to what goes on in the classroom. Children are curious about what their parents do in worship. They may not completely understand what is taking place. Some adults may not believe that children have the desire or the ability to relate to what takes place in a service. We should not be deterred. Taking the time to explain why we worship and why it is important is the first step in teaching a child how to worship. This practice is best modeled by parents and worship leaders.

We can provide worship services where children and parents come together in a setting where parents can help guide their children through a service. This takes a commitment on the part of the parent, the pastor, and the congregation to demonstrate patience and grace with children. If we keep sending them to their own program each week while "big church" is taking place, children will be deprived of the blessing of worshiping as a family and, in some cases, will not have the opportunity to learn the hymns, songs, and practices of the whole worshiping community.

I recall receiving a note from a mother who commented that on those Sundays when we have young children in church, we should only sing the songs they know. Her message was clear. "Let's not sing hymns." My response to her was, "How will children learn anything about traditional hymnody if we don't sing them on those few Sundays when your child is in 'big church'?"

As parents and worship leaders, we should help our children broaden their understanding and appreciation of worship. If we limit their exposure to the same 15 hymns and 10 praise choruses each week, we will be doing a great disservice to all ages. Children enjoy being challenged. This is true in sports, music, or worship. Teaching children about worship and how to worship requires a commitment and energy on the part of leaders/teachers. However, all of us receive great blessings and reap eternal benefits when we witness young children worshiping with their parents and the entire body of believers.

Teaching the Faith

Train up a child in the way he should go,
Even when he is old he will not depart from it.
(Prov. 22:6)

Some of the greatest blessings of my life occurred while growing up in a Christian home, attending eight years of Lutheran parochial school, and being raised in the church. I was always being taught the "faith" during those times. Whether it was my parents, my classroom teachers, or my pastors, I was taught the faith. Memory work, Bible stories, Confirmation, and church history were all part of my education and the development of my faith in Christ.

I am mindful that it was others who took on the responsibility of teaching me and helping me gain a greater understanding of theology, develop a Christian foundation, and come into a saving relationship with Jesus. I am indebted to many who guided me through my early years.

What does this have to do with worship? As worship leaders, you are in a similar position that my parents, teachers, and pastors were when they taught me the faith. You are in a place where you can teach the "faith of Christian worship" to those whom you serve and lead. Perhaps you are thinking, "that's the pastor's job" or "people already understand how we worship," or "I'm already too busy to take on another responsibility."

The truth is that you are likely the most qualified person on your church staff to be teaching about worship. Some seminary students are only required to take a few courses on worship theology and leading worship. This is understandable, given other course work that may be required to properly train our pastors. But this does not change the fact that worship is the heartbeat of the church. The late pastor Ray Ortlund often described worship as the first priority of the church. There is nothing more important than what we do when we worship God.

I am thankful for people such as William Lock, Robert Webber, Carla Waterman, and others from whom I have been privileged to learn. Without these individuals "teaching me the faith," I would not have had the opportunity to develop a theology of worship to share with those I have loved and served.

As worship leaders, you have the responsibility of carrying on this legacy of teaching in this important area. I am confident that if you interviewed people in your congregations, you would be surprised how many questions they have regarding the worship practices and theology in your church. Rather than seeing this as "one more thing to do," look upon it as an opportunity to deepen your congregation's worship life. Will this be a challenge? Absolutely! But it is an open window that truly does have eternal significance.

May God empower and lead you as you respond to this important call.

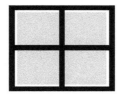

Windows on Preparing for Worship

Worshiping the Triune God is one of the highest callings and privileges we have as Christians. It is our response to what God has done for us through Jesus Christ. Worship must never be approached casually or in a spirit of "business as usual." In worship we come before the king of the universe. We read in Psalm 122:1, "I was glad when they said to me, 'Let us go to the house of the LORD.'" Preparing ourselves for worship is part of that gladness referred to in the psalm. Offering thoughtful prayer, focusing our thoughts, and anticipating the blessing we receive by being in the presence of Father, Son, and Holy Spirit are all parts of our preparation.

The 10 essays and devotional windows in this section provide principles and reflections focused on topics that help worship planners and leaders to be intentional in considering what elements are important in the shaping of a service. Whether it be the message, the reality of time constraints, the inclusion of visual components, the possibility of spontaneity, offering suggestions to a family in planning a funeral, or some other factor, everything that is considered and prepared for inclusion in worship must be brought before the Lord as our best offering and spiritual sacrifice.

God has wonderful and unique ways of revealing his plans for us in worship as we pour over the services that are before us. God's epiphanies come to us through prayer, study, and the words of colleagues. God is eager to use these gifts in combination with our talent and thoughts as we prepare and shape worship that will be given back to him by our congregations.

God will certainly do his part; we worship leaders, planners, and participants must do our part. May these windows of preparation help you achieve this goal in your ministry.

What's the Message?

For God so loved the world, that He gave His only begotten Son,
that whoever believes in Him shall not perish, but have eternal life.
(John 3:16)

One morning while driving to work, I was listening to a sermon on the radio. The preacher is well known and has quite a following. As with many religious programs, the sermon being aired was taken from a worship service at his church.

I listened for about 20 minutes. The preacher made many expository comments about the book of Revelation, how it relates to some writings in the Old Testament, and what it might mean for us and Planet Earth. I kept asking myself, "What is the message? What benefits are the listeners receiving that can help them in their spiritual walk?" For some, it might have been exactly what they needed to hear. For others, it might have raised more questions than answers.

Worship leaders and planners have important responsibilities. As you plan worship, there is always one question that needs to be answered: What is the message? Does the message being prepared (spoken, sung, chanted, or prayed) help our congregations grow in their understanding of God's love for us? Are the essentials of God's plan of salvation central to your worship services? Or are simple denominational tenets, traditions, and practices given the same importance or even overshadow the primary focus of worship?

Worship leaders should always be mindful of the message being given in worship, regardless of your tradition. Certainly, there are times for a variety of subjects that may range from the end times to stewardship. The focus of our message, however, should be the hope we have in Jesus. His cross and resurrection, and what they mean for us, must always be at the heart of the matter.

I encourage all of you who contribute to the planning of worship in your congregations to be mindful of the message that is being presented. You have a wonderful opportunity to share the Good News every week in what you do. It is a message that has eternal significance.

May you experience every joy as you serve God and lead God's people in the worship that you bring before him.

Where Did That Time Go?

Prepare your work outside
And make it ready for yourself in the field;
(Prov. 24:27a)

My father always told me that the older one gets, the more quickly time passes. Those who are in their 20s or 30s don't think too much about the brevity of life. Now that I am older and into my 70s, the reality of my dad's words ring truer and truer with me. Where did that time go?

I think about the 50-plus years I have spent in worship and music ministry. The challenge of allowing ample time for preparation is always a reality in professional and lay ministry. The "next thing" is always just around the corner whether it is a new choir season, a new sermon series, the next stewardship drive, or the next Sunday's sermon. Perhaps you are beginning a new choir season. Maybe it's September and your congregation is starting a new program year. Are you ready?

I remember the words of a middle school principal who once told one of her teachers, "You'd better have a plan. If you don't, the students do!" Our congregations, worship teams, and music groups are similar to the students. If you don't have a plan for them, they may have their own!

All of you who serve in leadership have the responsibility of investing yourself in prayer and preparation before you stand up in front of a choir, a congregation, or some other group in your church. In the busyness of your ministry, are you allowing ample time to prepare yourself? If the new choir season, program year, or sermon series has snuck up on you and you don't quite have all of the "i's" dotted and the "t's" crossed for the entire year, you can still recommit yourself to making it a priority to be ready for the next event.

The beginning of a new choir season or program year is when you need to step back, take a deep breath, and not be consumed by the enormity of the task that is before you. God takes us step by step, moment by moment, rehearsal by rehearsal, and service by service exactly where God wants to lead us. This doesn't mean that we can procrastinate. Rather, it means that we can move ahead in quiet confidence knowing that God will give us exactly what we need when we need it.

May your next service, program, rehearsal, or ministry opportunity be blessed by the Lord. May it be everything God would have it be. As you move through those times, be encouraged and enjoy the surprises God will have for you along the way.

A View into Heaven

Then I looked, and I heard the voices of many angels … saying with a loud voice,
"Worthy is the Lamb that was slain to receive power and riches and wisdom and might
and honor and glory and blessing."
(Rev. 5:11-12)

I have participated in many funerals during my ministry. On one occasion, I had the privilege of playing the organ for the service of a 70-year-old man who was a longtime member of the congregation where I was serving. James had sung in my choir for many years. He was a strong Christian and loved the Lord. His wife Betty also sang in the choir. Together, they had a wonderful understanding and appreciation of worship and music.

The funeral service James and Betty had planned reflected their love of music and the gospel message that music can convey. Our choir sang at the service. The congregation of about 200 came to the service ready to sing! It was a beautiful celebration of James' life and faith in the Savior.

James had a distinguished life of service to his church and community. His life touched many individuals, as was apparent by those who attended his funeral. As we gathered and sang the great hymns of the faith with enthusiasm and conviction, I thought to myself, "This is a mini-picture of what heavenly worship will be." To paraphrase Bryan Jeffrey Leech, the funeral worship service for James was a "glimpse of glory!" James' and Betty's preparation and planning helped to make that a reality.

Funerals and memorial services may be times of sadness over the loss of a loved one. For Christians, however, they are also an opportunity to give thanks and celebrate the life of one who placed their trust in the Lord. Whether the Word be spoken or sung, funerals also provide an opportunity for witness and worship.

Worship is not always intended to be upbeat. Oftentimes, a service can be a time of reflection, meditation, and communicating with God in an understated manner. Other times it can be uplifting, joyous, and celebrative—even at funerals. This was the case at James' service: it was just the way he wanted it!

Funerals as Worship

Surely goodness and lovingkindness will follow me all the days of my life,
And I will dwell in the house of the LORD forever.
(Ps. 23:6)

During one month of my ministry, I had the opportunity to do some serious thinking about funerals. Three deaths occurred within three weeks in the parish where I was serving. Each of the people who died was at a different stage in life.

The first funeral was for 63-year-old Sarah. She had suffered from cancer and was in significant pain for some time. The second service was for Hailey, an 11-year-old girl who was killed when her bicycle collided with a minivan. Her family was very involved in the life of the parish. Needless to say, Hailey's death shocked our entire church family and our community. The third funeral was for Barbara, who was well into her 80s. She had sung in the church choir for more than 50 years. Barbara was the perfect example of one who simply kept on going and loving the Lord until she died a peaceful death.

Different circumstances and conditions surrounded the death of each individual, but they shared a commonality: Sarah, Hailey, and Barbara all loved Jesus. Each had a service that celebrated their lives and that shared God's love with their families and the greater family. The Triune God was worshiped in each service, and the Easter gospel message of "He is risen!" was proclaimed.

No doubt, you have attended funerals or memorial services where the person was eulogized at length. Yet after the service, some attendees may have gone away with a sense of emptiness wondering whether the person who had died knew the Good Shepherd. Those who left Sarah, Hailey, and Barbara's services had no doubt that all three knew the Good Shepherd. Through the hymns, the anthems, the prayers, the spoken word, and the testimonies, those who were present met Jesus and heard of his love for Sarah, Hailey, and Barbara.

When you have the opportunity to be instrumental in preparing a funeral service with a family in your church, view it as "sacred time" to help the family and loved ones. Use your ministry gifts to help plan a service that will not only be a comfort and solace to the survivors, but also a witness to our desire to worship God in all of life's circumstances.

Seeing Is Believing

The hearing ear and the seeing eye,
The LORD has made both of them.
(Prov. 20:12)

I remember the first time we used projector screens in the congregation I was serving. The year was 2005. For some churchgoers this type of event would not have drawn much attention, but in our church it was a significant step. Installing screens in the sanctuary was a hard thing for some individuals in our parish to accept. I heard everything from, "It will be a distraction for me," to "What next? Follow the bouncing ball," to "It will destroy the solemnity of the sanctuary." For some, the addition of screens was viewed as an unnecessary departure from our "traditional" worship format.

Despite some of the concerns, many individuals saw the potential for sharing the gospel and enhancing corporate worship. They recognized that a new means of visualizing and communicating could be used alongside those practices that had served in the past and would continue to be used.

After installing the screens, we learned as individuals and as a congregation that many people retain and understand concepts and thoughts more clearly when they are able to visualize them rather than simply hear them. For visual learners, seeing something is how they comprehend. For some young children, images on stained glass windows are their first exposure to seeing the stories in the Bible come alive. Seeing really is believing!

I had reservations when discussions first began regarding installing screens in the sanctuary. Like many members of our congregation, I was raised in a very conservative setting that shaped and molded my perceptions regarding worship. However, upon seeing the use of screens in several different worship settings, I changed my mind and became convinced that the use of screens and multimedia programs can be a valuable tool. Through the years since 2005, we have witnessed how new forms of technology and multimedia are being used to enhance worship and share the gospel with those who were previously unreached. Indeed, the Covid-19 pandemic of 2020–2021 has forced churches to explore new ways of sharing worship services with their members through technology.

The gift of sight is one of God's great blessings to each one of us. If by seeing new images and words that allow us to commune with God both individually and corporately, we are able to draw closer to God, then we should do everything in our power to provide those tools to the people we serve.

The Many Moods of Worship

Bless the LORD, O my soul, and all that is within me, bless His holy name.
(Ps. 103:1)

One of the musical traditions often performed during the Christmas season is Robert Shaw's "The Many Moods of Christmas." Perhaps this is a work that you have programmed during your ministry. The idea of "the many moods of anything" raises questions: "What moods do people bring to worship? What moods do they experience in worship?"

The moods and feelings that are brought to worship are as diverse as those who bring them. Joy, disappointment, anger, mourning, doubt, peacefulness, grief, and hopefulness represent some of the moods people may carry into the presence of God. How can worship planners prepare for all of the possible feelings that may be present?

Our emotions and moods vary from day to day, and week to week. Recognizing this should be an affirmation to worship planners that attempting to address specific moods is difficult to achieve. Rather, the body of Christ is best served when those preparing the worship service consider using a variety of elements that minister to many different moods and emotions. This is not the same as trying to manipulate worshipers and their reactions by employing strategies that lack theological and historical integrity and underestimate what our Triune God can and does do in worship. God does not need that kind of "help!"

Some individuals believe that worship always needs to be "up"—never "down." This idea may be supported with a comment such as, "People don't want to be depressed." It is true that people do not want to be depressed by the worship they experience, but this does not mean that worship is always "up" if "up" is defined with terms such as fast, loud, and casual. I recall one pastor who would not permit music that was written in a minor key. Moods of contemplation, reflection, confession, prayer, silence, and even "minor keys" can convey many blessings to a worshiper regardless of the worship style. The personal realization of God's abiding presence, forgiveness, and love for us can be enhanced and strengthened by times of quiet solitude. It is in those moments when worshipers can benefit from the unplanned and unexpected "mood swings" in a worship service.

We must evaluate our own congregation. If you are serving in a church that has been historically very formal and rarely varies in its expressions in worship, it may be time to identify ways for individuals to experience a mood of spontaneity. Conversely, if you minister in a church where little attention is given to receiving the benefits of silence and a greater sense of formality, this may be the time to help your people experience those practices in a worship setting. I am not necessarily suggesting that you make a 180-degree turn in your order of worship. There are, however, wonderful resources and actions from many traditions available to help your church foster a deeper and even more meaningful worship experience that can minister to the moods of all.

Worship and the Art of Team Sports

And He gave some as apostles, and some as prophets, and some as evangelists,
and some as pastors and teachers … until we all attain to the unity of the faith,
and of the knowledge of the Son of God, to a mature man, to the measure
of the stature which belongs to the fullness of Christ.
(Eph. 4:11-13)

I enjoy playing golf. I am not good at it, but nevertheless I like going out and trying to survive 18 holes. Having experienced the challenge of trying to play the game gives me a huge appreciation for what professional golfers are able to do on a golf course. It is a challenging sport, one that requires a tremendous amount of discipline and practice. One thing that separates golf from other sports, however, is the fact that it is not a "team sport." Without diminishing what the great golfers do, they do not have the opportunity to demonstrate their skills in working with other team members.

Sometimes, the practice and discipline of corporate worship is mistaken for an individual "sport." How many times have we heard the comment from a disappointed or disgruntled congregation member, "I didn't get anything out of the worship service." It is at that point when individuals need to be reminded that corporate worship is a group activity. Worship is about the body of Christ coming together for a common purpose.

Much of what we hear and witness in today's culture is about the individual. Christian worship, however, is about the family of God joining together to offer their best to the Lord through a combined offering. Different individuals have different roles, similar to the players on an athletic team. If the right tackle fails to block the linebacker, the play breaks down. If the choir or praise team fails to prepare and focus, the assembly is distracted in their worship and the service is negatively affected.

All of us are "players" who have a part to play in the life of our worshiping congregation. Everyone and what they do is important, even if it is simply a unified acclamation to a prayer. We have all seen what happens when a player becomes disgruntled on a team. This one person's attitude hurts the other members of the team and their common goal of being successful. As worship leaders, it is our responsibility to affirm and encourage others and to continually teach them that the action of worship is not an "individual sport." Worship is a team activity that needs to have individuals rise above the question of "How does it make me feel?" The question, rather, needs to be, "Am I helping others to worship and glorify God by what I contribute to our worship?"

As individuals join together in their weekly corporate worship, the body of Christ is energized and edified, and God is given the glory and honor that he deserves.

Being Overprepared in Our Worship

And suddenly there came from heaven a noise like a violent rushing wind …
And they were all filled with the Holy Spirit and began to speak with other tongues,
as the Spirit was giving them utterance.
(Acts 2:2, 4)

The year was 1999. A lot was being written about the new millennium and the possible problems that might occur because of Y2K. Some people went to great lengths to prepare themselves for the worst-case scenario, while others completely disregarded the possibility of any kind of calamity. Obviously, we survived the dire predictions of Y2K.

Planning and preparing for worship can take on some of the same qualities that surrounded Y2K. There are those who do very little from week to week to prepare for worship, while in some denominations, the hymns and Scripture readings are predetermined for each Sunday. For some planners, this fact may convey a message that there is nothing else to prepare. In some traditions, the order of service does not change. There may be minimal thought given to planning portions of the service that allow for variety. Prayers, the reading of Scripture, the use of psalmody, and variation in how hymns and choruses are sung are some areas where different options and practices may be used. These portions of the service allow for creative and fresh approaches even in traditions where the order of service does not vary greatly.

The opposite of services where minimal preparation takes place are those worship times that are "overprepared." Of course, details must be given attention. In some situations, however, where services are scripted and timed out to the final minute, there is no consideration of or allowance for the possibility of a "Pentecost moment." There *are* times when God wants to surprise us in worship! Perhaps as leaders and worshipers, those moments are missed because we are more focused on what has been planned for God rather than on what God has planned for us.

God is a God of order. He wants us to be prepared when we meet him in worship. The building of the Ark of the Covenant and tabernacle in Exodus, the instructions regarding animal sacrifices in Leviticus, and the details regarding the dedication of the wall in Nehemiah give affirmation to God's desire for orderliness in worship. Yet, God is also a God of surprises who can show us new things and come to us in different ways whenever we least expect it.

As you think about worship and how you plan it, be mindful that worship is what we do in response to God's love for us in Jesus. Be prepared, but don't miss those opportunities for your people to meet the Lord in surprising and beautiful ways.

Good News! Good News!

For I am not ashamed of the gospel, for it is the power of God
for salvation to everyone who believes . . .
(Rom. 1:16)

Years ago there was a television program called *Gomer Pyle USMC* starring Jim Nabors as Gomer Pyle, a raw recruit in the Marine Corps. You may recall that Gomer was a little different than the other recruits. When he was excited about something, he would always exclaim, "Good news! Good news!"

How excited are you about the real Good News? What is your energy level when you are doing your part in sharing the gospel in a worship setting? What is your mindset as you plan, prepare, lead, and participate in the weekly worship time in your church?

Keep in mind that the weekly worship time is always a "new song" (Ps. 33:3). Although it retells age-old truths, worship is always a new and fresh experience. The worshiping congregation is never the same group from the prior week. The circumstances in worship vary. Even if your order of service is basically the same every week, the themes, music, prayers, and spoken word must be approached with an understanding that there will be new thoughts and insights that can emerge.

As you think about sharing the Good News, do not hesitate to use means and expressions that have been successful in previous worship services. Using a prayer, a chorus, or a response does not guarantee that everyone was present on a previous occasion when it might have been included. Repetition in our liturgies, either formal or informal, has been at the heart of Christian worship for centuries.

When you plan and lead worship, remember that everything is not dependent upon you. St. Augustine said, "Pray as though everything depended on God. Work as though everything depended on you." After you have done your part to the best of your ability, allow God's Holy Spirit to be in charge. Too often, the "success" of a worship service is based upon our feelings rather than the work that the Holy Spirit has accomplished. You may never know all of the "success" stories in people's lives that occur because of the work of the Spirit during the service.

"Good News! Good News!" This is at the heart of what worship planners and leaders do: You proclaim the gospel, offer praise and thanks to God, and worship with others with an anticipation of what God's Spirit can and will do. Be encouraged in your ministry as you prepare and plan for the most important hour of the week—that hour when God's people meet and share in the "Good News!"

When Sunday Seems to Come Every Other Day

Build up, build up, prepare the way,
Remove every obstacle out of the way of My people.
(Isa. 57:14)

Those who have the privilege and responsibility of planning and leading worship are continually aware of the challenges involved. Preparing services that reflect freshness, new energy, and elements that are appropriate to the season of the church year or to the current thematic emphasis is an ongoing task. This challenge, when combined with other important responsibilities, can contribute to a sense of never having enough time.

The late Howie Stevenson, former minister of music at the First Evangelical Free Church in Fullerton, California, said: "For worship leaders, Sunday seems to come every three days. Trying to bring freshness and newness to worship constantly challenges us."[1] Worship leaders understand the demands that continually pull at them as they faithfully do their best in planning the most important weekly event in the life of their church. How can you approach this reality so that you are successful in this area?

If you serve in a church that uses the lectionary or where your pastor has planned out the Scripture readings and sermons for the foreseeable future, thank the Lord. You already have the most important element needed to help you in planning ahead and finding time to include fresh ideas into your services. If you are in a church where Scripture readings or sermon topics are planned from week to week, do all that you can to change that practice. Be encouraged to pray, seek advice from your peers, and work with your pastor to achieve an understanding of the importance of the need to receive information far enough in advance so that the congregation's worship can be all that the Lord would have it to be. There may be some instances where the failure to provide readings or topics is simply a time management matter. In those cases, it may be helpful for you to offer to assist your pastor in selecting some of the readings.

Developing your own "file of new ideas" is a valuable tool in being able to work ahead. The best sources of new ideas and resources can be other music ministers and worship leaders, periodicals, conferences, and visiting other churches. Keep your list of ideas current. You may not use a certain idea this month, but it might be useful in six months. Do not be afraid to repeat ideas and practices that work. If something was successful nine months ago, use it again if it is appropriate. In our mobile society, it is likely that some worshipers will be experiencing the "new" idea for the first time. Be confident in ideas and practices that work for you. Finally, as you think about your worship planning and preparation, develop a long-range plan and vision to expand those ideas. Hopefully, by using some of these suggestions you won't meet yourself coming and going. Then, Sunday will come every seventh day rather than every other day!

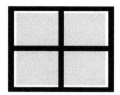

Windows on the Church Year and Worship

How many times have you experienced events in your life that you thoroughly enjoyed? It might have been a vacation, the wedding of a family member or friend, a reunion, or some other occasion. After the activities came to an end, you took some time to reflect upon them. You may have taken some pictures along the way that allowed you to recall the fond memories from your journey. You might have reminisced or even wished that you could return in time and relive the activities that brought you joy. However, you realized that the hope of returning was only a dream and, at best, a memory. You cannot go back in time!

The church year allows for just the opposite: You *can* go back in time and remember, recall, and reenact many of the events of God's story. In celebrating the church year, you immerse yourself in the biblical story. By making an annual journey to the manger, the Mount of Transfiguration, the open tomb, and numerous other sites and locales, you can hear the majestic voice of our Heavenly Father, witness the reality of the Risen Christ, and experience the power of the Holy Spirit.

The 12 essays included in this section provide a roadmap that take you from the voice of one "crying in the wilderness" to the coronation and recognition of Christ the King, in addition to other significant events that occur between the bookends of the church year. Using the church year to guide your congregation through the events in the life of Jesus and to nurture their spiritual growth is a powerful way to experience the Holy Spirit's faith-building work.

May your excursion through the church year open new windows for you and your congregation.

Leaf Raking and Advent Wreaths

Lift up your heads, O gates, … that the King of glory may come in!
(Ps. 24:7)

There are a lot of oak trees around my house. They are magnificent! When I stand on my deck and look into my backyard, it is as though I have my own private forest. The foliage creates a beautiful canopy of green. There is, however, a downside to this scenario. With the enjoyment of the trees also comes the reality of picking up thousands of acorns and raking up a similar number of leaves. Each fall when I go out into the backyard to work, it is a reminder that we are rapidly approaching colder temperatures and shorter days. It also brings to mind that we are nearing the "best time" of the year.

Thanksgiving is a wonderful holiday and time that can be used to pause and remember the blessings we have experienced and continue to realize each day. With each leaf that is raked comes the reminder that we are quickly approaching the season of Advent, a time of personal and spiritual preparation for the coming of Jesus. From a personal perspective, Advent is my favorite season of the church year. Great hymns, meaningful prayers, the "O" antiphons, the color blue, the prophetic readings from Isaiah … wow! All of these elements give us an opportunity to reflect and slow down as we get ready for the One who will be coming. Those who serve in full-time ministry need times to slow down and get ready. One friend has referred to these moments as "mini vacations."

I suspect that the people in your congregation also need mini vacations. They need to be able to come to an "oasis" in the middle of their hurried week, to stop, and "smell the Advent wreath." You can give them no better gift than to create worship environments and settings that are countercultural and will allow them to leave a service recognizing that they have been able to slow down and reflect upon those things that really matter in life. The four Sundays of Advent provide a wonderful opportunity to do this.

Consider making your Sundays of Advent different from normal Sunday morning worship experiences. Talk with your pastor about helping to provide a worship setting that will encourage your congregation to experience the quietness that God encourages us to seek.

The Lord commands us to "be still." When we are still, we are able to listen and hear God speak to us. All of us need to hear God's word and prepare our hearts as we contemplate the coming of Jesus.

The next time you are raking leaves, take time to be quiet, listen, and think about how you will help your people "smell the Advent wreath."

A Season of Waiting

… For You I wait all the day.
(Ps. 25:5)

Some time ago, I had an occasion to be reading Psalm 25 with a group of friends. As we were reading the text, I was struck by the words of verse 5: "Lead me in Your truth and teach me, For You are the God of my salvation; For You I wait all the day." These final words, "For You I wait all the day," reminded me of a truth with which many of us struggle, namely, that the Christian life is about waiting. Our human nature does not like to wait. It's similar to the old saying, "I want patience, and I want it *now!*"

Why do we struggle with waiting? It is because of our human nature, which is not the way God intended it to be. It's broken. Our lack of patience is part of that brokenness. We cannot fix it by ourselves, but God has provided the cure in His Son, Jesus.

Advent marks the start of a new church year. It is that time on the liturgical calendar when we focus on the coming of Jesus. By its very nature, Advent requires us to wait. For some, the waiting may be a time of sorrow, loneliness, or isolation. For others, it may be a time of joy, excitement, or anticipation. Whatever our circumstances in life, Advent is a microcosm of the total Christian walk. It is a time of waiting.

God's plan has always included times of waiting. Abraham and Sarah waited for Isaac. The Israelites waited in Egypt and Babylon. Simeon and Anna lived an "Advent life" as they waited to see the Savior. God places us in "Advent moments" to shape us and deepen our dependency on him.

Even as we "wait" for the Lord during this season, we can be certain that he is already with us through any times of uncertainty we might be facing. In the midst of waiting through difficult times and challenges and asking when they will be over, Jesus is with us now. Because he is with us, we can define our life by the life of Jesus. We do not experience anything that he has not already confronted.

Advent *is* a time of waiting. Yet, it is also a time of quiet assuredness and faith. As we wait for Jesus to return, we can say with assurance that he is already here!

"You are the God of my salvation; For You I wait all the day" (Ps. 25:5). As we wait for the Lord and his plans for us, we do so, knowing that he *is* with us right now.

God bless you and your times of Advent waiting.

Advent Continues

I am coming quickly; hold fast what you have,
so that no one will take your crown.
(Rev. 3:11)

If you read this at the beginning of a new calendar year, you will have just come through the Advent and Christmas seasons and will be moving into the season of Epiphany. It seems as though we all move much too quickly from one season to another, both liturgically and chronologically. Once we get through December, we are "done" with Advent and Christmas and ready to move on to the next thing.

The whole purpose of Advent is to prepare for the coming of Christ, both as a baby and as king of the universe. We spend four weeks doing that. Then we celebrate Christmas, perhaps for 12 days, before moving on to the next thing.

Pragmatically, we think in terms of short-term and long-term goals and ideas when it comes to planning things programmatically. But what do you take with you from the seasons you have just completed when it comes to applying them to your personal life and the lives of those you serve?

How does the reality of Christ returning affect how you plan worship the other 48 weeks of the year? How much time do you take to think about the application of the reality that he is coming again, and that it may not happen during the four weeks of Advent?

While I was writing these thoughts, I learned that the spouse of one of my dearest and most treasured friends had gone to be with the Lord. It was a sad time for those of us who mourned her death. However, for her, she was ready and prepared for Advent. She knew that the Lord was coming for her, and she had no fears about leaving this world.

As a worship leader or planner, do you think about the eternal significance of what you are doing and how it prepares your congregation to be ready for heavenly worship when the Lord comes for them? This intention should be at the forefront of your thinking and planning every week whether it is Advent, Christmas, Epiphany, Lent, Easter, Pentecost, or Ordinary Time.

Several years ago, I had a little accident in my backyard and took a fall. I was fine and no worse for wear. As I was tumbling over and seeing my life flash before my eyes, however, I was reminded as to how quickly our personal Advent with the Lord can occur.

As you think about those you serve, you have the opportunity and responsibility to keep reminding them that Advent is an ongoing reality for all of them. Jesus has come. Jesus is coming again. And Jesus continues to come in the midst of his people and the world.

Who Am I?

But who do you say that I am?
(Matt. 16:15)

I remember a childhood game where the players would try to guess the identity of an individual. Each participant would be allowed to ask one question in the hope of combining enough information with other players that would ultimately lead to revealing the name of the "mystery person." Sometimes the puzzle could be solved after two or three questions. Other times it required additional information. On other occasions the mystery person's identity was never discovered.

The season of Epiphany is similar to that game. Throughout the post-Christmas time, clue after clue is revealed that shows the identity of Jesus. The visit of the magi, Jesus' baptism in the Jordan River, his turning water into wine during the wedding at Cana, Jesus' own proclamation of fulfilling the Isaiah 61:1 prophecy, and, of course, his transfiguration are some of the examples during the Epiphany season that help us answer the question, "Who am I?"

Some people are able to answer that question quickly after receiving the answer to one or two "clues." Others are still asking the question. And, unfortunately, there are those who either have no interest or who have stopped seeking the answer to the question altogether.

During the Epiphany season, all of us have the opportunity to revisit the "revelations" of Jesus' identity by hearing and revisiting all of the accounts shared in Scripture and in worship. We have the chance to be renewed after a busy Christmas season. This renewal can be used to share Jesus with those who may still be asking the question, "Who is Jesus?"

May each of you continue to meet Jesus in both old and new ways as he continues to reveal himself not only during the Epiphany season, but also in your daily walk throughout the year. May you share in his "Epiphany Light" and continue to marvel at those ways as he answers the question, "Who am I?"

Epiphany: A Time of Light

. . . God is Light, and in Him there is no darkness at all.
(1 John 1:5)

Have you ever wondered about the first spoken words recorded in Scripture? "Then God said, 'Let there be light'" (Gen. 1:3). The nature and characteristics of light must have great importance for it to have been created immediately after the creation of the heavens and the earth (Gen. 1:1). Can you imagine what our world would be like without light?

The Gospel readings for the season of Epiphany (January 6 through Transfiguration Sunday) are bookended by two lessons that include light as a major component. The Feast of the Epiphany includes the brightness of the star that guided the Wise Men (Matt. 2:2). The narratives of Jesus' transfiguration speak of how his garments became "radiant" (Mark 9:3) and how his clothing became "white and flashing like lightning" (Luke 9:29). The events included in the other Gospel readings for the Season of Epiphany also "shed light" on Jesus and his ministry.

Throughout Scripture, "light" is mentioned on many occasions. We are instructed to "walk as children of Light" (Eph. 5:8). Jesus refers to himself as "the Light of the world" (John 8:12). The apostle John includes Light as an important part of his first epistle.

Throughout the ages, the poets and musicians of the church have grasped the importance of light in their writings and hymnody. For example, these hymns and songs scatter brightness upon Jesus, the Light of the World, and his ministry of redemption and reconciling love for us:

• "O Morning Star, How Fair and Bright"
• "As with Gladness Men of Old"
• "Brightest and Best of the Stars of the Morning"
• "I Want to Walk as a Child of the Light"
• "Shine, Jesus, Shine"

Epiphany is a season of light, a time when we are given a brighter understanding and vision for the Light that Jesus offers us. Just as important, it is a time when we can become empowered and equipped to be Christ's Light in a dark world and share it 365 days a year. We have a wonderful message to share. We have words that can change people's lives and help to heal hurting souls.

Do not allow your Epiphany season to be limited to six or seven weeks in the calendar year. Rather, take the "Light" that comes to you and give it away every day. As the old gospel song says, "This little light of mine, I'm going to let it shine." Share the Light of Jesus that has been freely given to you.

Remembering Past Worship Traditions

I remember the days of old;
I meditate on all Your doings . . .
(Ps. 143:5)

Mid-week Lenten services are a time-honored tradition in many Lutheran churches. As a young boy, I remember attending the Wednesday night services during the six weeks of Lent. In my congregation, it was something that everyone did. As a matter of fact, there was a period of time that because of the high attendance, two identical services were held—one at 6:30 and the other at 7:45.

It is safe to say that the attendance figures are significantly lower now than they were in the 1960s and 1970s. People are finding new ways to occupy their time. The fact that some individuals and families no longer utilize many Lenten disciplines is a sad reality. What is encouraging, though, is that regardless of the changes in our culture, some churches still return to their roots and offer those worship opportunities that have helped to shape many individuals' faith journeys. There are those people who long for, and continue to identify with, the practices and traditions that helped form them in their faith and worship habits. By making an annual return to that six-week period of Lenten services, individuals can experience renewal and inspiration.

What is a mid-week Lenten service for some may be a Wednesday night prayer service or a Sunday night revival service for others. Whatever form the "tradition" or worship practice takes on is not the issue. The focus is that believers continue to visit and revisit those worship practices that helped to nurture them in their formative years.

In a day and age when some people clamor for change for change's sake, others are finding their renewal and inspiration at the oasis of familiarity. They find strength in those things that have guided them along the way. Does this mean that we don't look for and explore new ways and opportunities to create new traditions? Absolutely not! We continue to seek, find, and develop new expressions that allow all of God's people to come into his presence for the purpose of worshiping and honoring him. The church has done this for centuries and will continue to do so.

However, in the rush and eagerness to find new ways to do liturgy (the work of the people), let us not forget that much of what made us the worshipers we are today can still be an important part of our journey. There is much to be said for those quiet mid-week "Lenten service moments," the Wednesday night prayer services, and the Sunday night revival services. They have a profound way of reminding us who we are and how God has been with us throughout the years.

40 Days In, 40 Days Of?

Now on the first day of the week Mary Magdalene came early to the tomb, while it was still dark, and saw the stone already taken away from the tomb.
(John 20:1)

Lent … that 40-day period when we remember the solemn events in the life of Jesus. Have you ever taken the time to reflect upon the significance of the number 40 in the Bible? How often does it appear? Recall these examples: Noah and his family endured the great flood for 40 days and nights; Moses spent 40 years in Egypt, 40 years being prepared by God, and 40 years leading the children of Israel; and Jesus spent 40 days in the wilderness and 40 days after his resurrection prior to his ascension. Periods of 40 days and years are important in the Bible and in the life of the church as you plan worship for the season of Lent.

Starting with Ash Wednesday and counting the number of days until Easter Sunday, you will quickly discover that there are more than 40 days. That is not a mistake. In establishing a church year and liturgical calendar, the early church leaders were wise to not include Sundays in counting the number of days for Lent. It was intentional. Their plan helps us to remember that even as we move through the 40-day season of Lent, we need to think in terms of the Sundays *in* Lent as opposed to the Sundays *of* Lent.

You might be asking, "What's the difference?" The difference is the theology of the Resurrection. Every Sunday—whether in Advent, Epiphany, Lent, or Ordinary Time—is a celebration and remembrance of the Resurrection. It is a "little Easter." This reality must shape how we plan and lead worship times with those whom we are called to lead and serve.

One of the hallmarks of the Lutheran tradition is that the congregation is always sent out from worship with the hope of the gospel. Individuals are not left searching for "the answer." The answer is always found in the hope we have in the Resurrection. When the Resurrection guides your planning, you can be certain that you will be observing and celebrating the Sundays *in* Lent rather than falling into a time of focusing upon the Sundays *of* Lent.

There are 40 days other than the Sundays to call and invite your people into the Lenten disciplines and practices. These opportunities are important and necessary. Provide your congregation with times to participate in mid-week services or moments of personal meditation and devotion. Then when you gather as the body of Christ, you can remember, celebrate, and apply to every life what Jesus has done for each of us through his glorious resurrection.

Christ is risen! He is risen, indeed! Alleluia!

Easter: 365

. . . that I may know Him and the power of His resurrection . . .
(Phil. 3:10)

Easter Sunday is sometimes referred to as a "moveable feast." There is no set date. Many of us have heard people say, "Easter comes early this year," or "Easter comes late this year." As one who spent most of my adult life planning worship and music in a variety of congregational settings, I can assure you that I always preferred it when Easter came "late." Preparing music and worship for Advent and Christmas and then turning around and immediately starting preparations for an early Easter in March always caused more stress than when Easter arrived later in April. I always appreciated having a few more weeks to catch my breath and get ready.

In the Christian life, Easter does not come early or late. Rather, Easter is every day! Each year, the dates will vary when the Resurrection of Jesus is celebrated. Whether it is March 26 or April 19 does not matter. What matters is that God's people come together and collectively celebrate the greatest event in the history of the universe.

Easter, in the life of a Christian, is much more than a single date on the calendar. As followers of Jesus, we live in the power and hope of the open tomb every day of the year. It is Easter—365! We *are* the Easter people! We live with a certainty and assurance based upon the fact that because Jesus has overcome death and sin, we too overcome death and sin.

Even during the season of Lent, the church continues to remember the events that led to the Resurrection of Jesus. While remembering those solemn events, we continue to live each day in the power of the Risen Christ. The church year in its tradition, thought, and wisdom intentionally continues the celebration of Easter for six weeks following Easter Sunday up until Pentecost. This ancient practice helps us to recognize that Easter goes beyond a single date. During those six weeks, we continue to sing the hymns and songs of Easter. We join with the voices of the saints through the ages in proclaiming, "Christ is risen! He is risen, indeed! Alleluia!"

Singing an Easter hymn or reading an Easter text in worship throughout the year is a good thing to do. That's what Easter people are all about. It is the body of Christ celebrating the power and the hope of Jesus' victory. It is God's people celebrating Easter—365!

Better Late Than Never

Blessed be the God and Father of our Lord Jesus Christ,
who according to His great mercy has caused us to be born again to a living hope
through the resurrection of Jesus Christ from the dead.
(1 Pet. 1:3)

The previous "window" emphasized the truth of Easter—365. Christians around the world place their hope in the reality of Jesus' resurrection. Some individuals spend their entire life with the knowledge of this truth and live every day in the power of and promise of Jesus' victory over death.

They may have come to faith in a variety of ways. Depending upon their beliefs and traditions, it may have been at their baptism, a personal testimony at the age of accountability, or some other faith-event early in their life. The knowledge, reality, and blessing of Easter has always been a part of who they are. For these people, Easter comes "early." They live with the assurance that because Jesus lives, they will live.

For others, Easter and its power comes later in life. Perhaps they were not raised in a Christian home or did not have any interaction with Sunday School or church in their formative years. Their first introduction to the reality of the open tomb may have come when they experienced a life-event that caused them to reflect and reexamine their future without a hope. They may have met Jesus and witnessed his resurrection when their spouse or friend shared the message of the Savior and his resurrection.

Still, others meet the Risen Christ in their final years or even final moments of their life. They may have gone through life without thinking about an eternal relationship with God. But through the prayers and love of others, these "seniors" come to a place where they recognize the living Christ and all that he offers. For these individuals, Easter may come in the last moments of this life—but it does come! For them, it is indeed a blessing of eternal significance that Easter comes better late than never.

As worship planners and leaders, do not forget that God never gives up on people. God is always reaching out with open hands and words of invitation. May your times of worship continually reflect the hope of Easter. Without Easter, nothing else matters in the eternal scheme of things. Allow worship times to convey God's love for us. Your congregation will always have attendees for whom Easter has come, Easter is in the process of coming, or Easter will come at a time in the future.

Because he lives, we live: This is Jesus' promise to us. Thanks be to God!

Hearing the Good Shepherd's Voice

I am the good shepherd; the good shepherd lays down His life for the sheep.
(John 10:11)

The Fourth Sunday of Easter is also known as "Good Shepherd Sunday" in some traditions. In the lectionary, John 10:11-18 and Psalm 23 are the assigned gospel and psalm reading, respectively.

There are a number of hymns that use Psalm 23 as their inspiration. One of them is "The Lord's My Shepherd, I'll Not Want," from *The Psalms of David in Meeter*, 1650. This hymn was my father's favorite, and it was sung at his funeral. It brings back many memories whenever it is sung during our worship services. Other hymns based on Psalm 23 include "Savior, Like a Shepherd Lead Us" and "The King of Love My Shepherd Is."

During our times of challenges, uncertainty, and "valley days," it can become very easy to focus on our frustrations. They can be times when our faith is tested and stretched. At times like this, the enemy makes every attempt to distract us from following the Good Shepherd. Satan will use every type of negative situation to tempt us to turn our eyes away from Jesus and follow a different voice. Perhaps it is a voice of discouragement, self-pity, or doubt. When these temptations come before us, it is the time to remember the words of Jesus in John 10: ". . . he goes ahead of them, and the sheep follow him because they know his voice" (v. 4).

Psalm 23:4 reminds and assures us that even though we walk through the valley of the shadow of death—or discouragement, or illness, or whatever we may be facing—we do not need to be afraid. Our Good Shepherd is with us.

We are living in challenging times. But we also live in the Easter season, every day of our life. We have a Good Shepherd who has overcome the greatest challenge of all. He has conquered sin, death, and the devil and everything associated with those things. We need not fear. We are the Easter people, the sheep of his flock. Therefore, we can confidently sing: "Goodness and mercy all my life shall surely follow me; And in God's house forevermore my dwelling place shall be."

Ordinary Time: An Oxymoron

Preach the word; be ready in season and out of season;
reprove, rebuke, exhort, with great patience and instruction.
(2 Tim. 4:2)

If you serve in a denomination that observes the church year, once Pentecost Sunday has occurred, the church moves into Ordinary Time. In previous lectionaries and church calendars, this season was referred to as the Sundays after Pentecost. It is the longest season of the church year, lasting from the Sunday after Pentecost until Christ the King Sunday. While there are many stories and experiences from Jesus' life reflected in the lectionary readings to help us shape worship in the first half of the church year (Advent through Pentecost), the readings after Pentecost do not generally deal with events in the life of Jesus. Rather, they deal with topics that help us nurture and grow in our faith. During this season we can adopt a mentality of "ordinary time" when it comes to worship planning.

As a worship planner, it is important to avoid this "ordinary" type of thinking, however. When we move into the summer months, it may become difficult to think about how to fill the worship times with special music, summer choirs, special sermons, and the like. We may be tempted to look for ways to "survive" the summer months. If we are not careful, our worship services can indeed become ordinary.

Christian worship is never ordinary. Whether it is Easter Sunday, and the sanctuary is bursting at the seams with people, or it is the third Sunday in August and your church is on the "summer schedule" with only one service, worship must always be the most important priority for the body of Christ. Worship is that time when we come into the presence of God and have a divine encounter. There is nothing ordinary about coming into his presence. Whenever we are in God's presence, his life-changing power and action are at work. The Lord is always ready to transform us spiritually, regardless if it is Easter Sunday or the third Sunday in August! Our faithfulness as worship leaders in returning to the spiritual habits that define us are a powerful resource to draw upon in planning worship.

We must never lose sight of this reality. Ordinary Time must never be approached with a spirit of casualness. Is it easier to plan for the "big Sunday"? Is it easier to get your musicians excited and motivated at those times? Is it easier for the pastor to preach on those Sundays? The answer is a resounding "yes" to all of these questions. It is in the faithfulness and sweat of the ordinary times, however, that we experience the encouraging power of the Holy Spirit as we keep listening for what God would have us do in those Sunday worship times.

I encourage you to trust in God's promises and persevere as you labor through the times when the going seems to be the most difficult. God is faithful to give you what you need when you need it. God will not let you down.

Remembering and Looking Ahead

Therefore, since we have so great a cloud of witnesses surrounding us . . .
(Heb. 12:1)

One of the many blessings I have experienced in 50 years of ministry is serving in churches that observe the church, or liturgical, year. In the church year there are opportunities to continually remember, celebrate, and look ahead to many of the significant events in the life of Christ and to other important occasions in the life and history of the church.

Two of the most important observances in the liturgical church year fall during the month of November. They are All Saints' Day and Christ the King Sunday. While All Saints' Day is always a fixed date (November 1), Christ the King always falls on the final Sunday of the church year prior to the First Sunday of Advent.

It is ironic how these two observances fall so closely to one another. With All Saints' Day, we have the opportunity to "remember." Christ the King Sunday allows us to "look ahead." In both instances, there are moments to give thanks to God for what he has done through those who have gone on to the "larger life" and for what we can look forward to when Jesus, the King of kings, returns to take us with him. In a real sense, these two observances bookend the Christian life for all of us who live each day remembering *and* looking ahead—all the while being in the present.

I am reminded every day of the wonderful passage from Hebrews 12: "Therefore, since we have so great a cloud of witnesses surrounding us ..." (v. 1). We are being encouraged by the saints as we move through our lives in anticipation of the return of the King! As we are encouraged by those who have come before us, may we do the same for those with whom we live. That is how we live as part of God's story. We encourage, support, and love one another. We worship together as the body of Christ. We are a community, remembering those before us, looking forward at what is to come, and living in the present as God leads us each day.

May your memories of the past and your hopes for the future be an encouragement each day as you live in the present for the Lord.

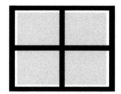

Windows on Worship That Transforms Lives

I remember a story about an annual meeting that was taking place in a local church. The properties committee was presenting its report and noted that some of the lights in the sanctuary had burned out and would need to be "changed." One older gentleman immediately stood up and shouted, "Change? Change?"

Using the word "change" in a church setting can present some challenges. Changing the light bulbs, carpet color, or service times is one kind of change. Another kind of change—and far more important—is spiritual change.

When we talk about spiritual change or transformation in worship, we are talking about God's action that affects people's lives. For some, they consider modifying their views on a social issue or developing more patience as a type of personal transformation. What God offers in worship is far more important.

The 10 essays in this final section speak to the matter of spiritual transformation and how your participation and commitment to Christian worship can lead to significant spiritual, and in some cases, physical change in your life.

From asking ourselves, "What are our expectations in worship," to recognizing our personal needs and the blessings we can receive in worship, these 10 windows address questions and issues in our life that we all need to consider, for example:

- What do you hope to receive in worship?
- How's the health in your church?
- Do you have an awareness of God's presence in worship?

God is in the "change business." By considering these questions, you make yourself available for God's life-changing and transforming love and power.

As you read each essay, may you recognize and experience that presence and power in your worship life and the lives of the people you serve.

What Do We Hope to Receive?

For the LORD takes pleasure in His people;
He will beautify the afflicted ones with salvation.
(Ps. 149:4)

Have you ever asked yourself the question, "What motivates people to attend a worship service?" There are likely as many answers as there are individuals who attend. For some, coming to church is a habit they have had since childhood. Others may be motivated by a Spirit-directed desire to interact and commune with the living God. Some people attend because they have been invited by a friend. Whatever the reason, the critical fact is that they *are* present and there is the potential for a life change.

More important than what motivates people is the question of what people expect to receive from their worship experience. How many people attend a service expecting to be different when they leave than when they came? This is a critical question that we who have a role in planning and leading worship must continually ask. Do people come to worship with a minimal expectation of what God will do for them in the service? How many attend with an attitude of "business as usual"? Some individuals may arrive without even considering the possibility of experiencing a life-changing moment in the context of worship.

Someone's expectations of what can occur in worship or what they will personally allow to happen to them in a service can be a reflection of the condition of their heart. Some people may come to worship with no desire to experience the closeness of God or the fresh breath of the Spirit. They can be hesitant to become vulnerable and allow the nearness of God to change areas of their lives that need to be changed. However, as a worship leader and teacher, you have the privilege, the duty, and the responsibility to continually present your congregation with the powerful message of the life-changing gospel. You have the opportunity, out of love, to stretch people to be open to what God wants to do for them in worship. God desires for everyone to be forgiven, made whole, and be restored from the brokenness caused by the condition and consequences of sin.

Worship should never be routine. Be an agent of change who encourages your people to come to worship every week expecting to be different when they leave than when they arrived. May that be your mission and ministry as you continue to serve the Lord by sharing the gospel of redemptive and healing love in Jesus.

Transformational Worship

Bless the LORD … Who pardons all your iniquities, Who heals all your diseases; Who redeems your life from the pit, Who crowns you with lovingkindness and compassion; Who satisfies your years with good things, So that your youth is renewed like the eagle.
(Ps. 103:2-5)

No doubt, some of you experienced the "worship wars" of the 1980s and 1990s, and to some extent the first few years of the 21st century. During that period of time, those who were involved in various worship leadership positions heard many of the buzz words associated with Christian worship in the local church setting. Terms such as traditional, contemporary, postmodern, Gen-X, blended, intergenerational, and numerous other descriptions were used to try and define different worship styles.

I have tried to avoid words such as traditional and contemporary simply because they mean different things to different people. For some, defining a specific type of worship has been about music styles. For others, it has been about organs versus praise bands. Some define traditional as "liturgical," while others use "non-liturgical" to describe contemporary—although strictly speaking, every church has a liturgy.

As Martin Luther would ask, "What does this mean?" The answer is that many worship planners and leaders struggle with labels in terms of attempting to describe what they do in worship, rather than simply drawing upon a variety of historic and recent resources to provide a setting that gives God a means to use in meeting people wherever they may be spiritually. It is not about contemporary or traditional. Rather, it is about worship that transforms the lives of those who meet the Lord in that setting.

One question remains. "Do you expect to be different when you leave worship than when you came?" If you come expecting to be changed because you have been in the presence of the living God, then you *will* be different! You will be changed. Jesus said, "For where two or three have gathered together in My name, I am there in their midst" (Matt. 18:20). When Jesus is present, things happen! The change may not be identical for each person, but the individual transformation will be specifically designed for each worshiper by the Holy Spirit, the divine "agent of change."

While a student at the Robert E. Webber Institute for Worship Studies, I heard a memorable lecture on Holy Communion given by Dr. Carla Waterman. Speaking of the benefits each of us in our varied denominations receive from the Lord's Supper, she said, "There is no doubt that God meets us at the table. The question among different traditions is, 'how?'"[1]

We are transformed in worship, not because of our worship preferences or personal understanding of every theological doctrine, but because of God's presence and promises. I pray that your worship services with your congregations will be times when lives and hearts receive God's transforming love and power.

What Are We Seeking?

And He said to the woman, "Your faith has saved you; go in peace."
(Luke 7:50)

Worship leaders and planners work and deal with a variety of people. It is safe to presume that some of those individuals bring traits and life experiences that are quite different from each other. This is one of the realities of serving in the church.

When we consider worship and all it includes, we are often brought back to the possibility that not everyone appreciates what may or may not occur in our congregational worship. Some people look for one thing, while others hope for something entirely different. There are also those who aren't sure what they are seeking.

But almost everyone is seeking one thing in common when they come to worship, whether they realize it or not. It is not if the choir sings a certain anthem, or if someone says "hello," or if you get to sing your favorite hymn. It is being at peace with God and knowing that God is at peace with us.

The Gospel of Luke shares the story of the woman who came to dinner uninvited and washed Jesus' feet with her tears and dried his feet with her hair (7:36-49). Clearly, the woman had a "reputation" and was not at peace with who she was, let alone at peace with God. Everyone in the room knew who she was. Jesus was the only one who welcomed her. The woman never spoke a word. There was no need for her to say anything. Her tears and actions spoke for her. Jesus knew what she needed. If you read the entire story, you will see that Jesus did two things: He forgave her sins and *then* said to her, "Go in peace." Therein lies the answer to the question of what she was looking for—God's peace. She left with the assurance that she had it.

Take a moment and think about what happens in your worship services. Different traditions may vary. In the Lutheran tradition, services conclude with the Aaronic blessing found in Numbers 6:24-26: "The LORD lift up His countenance on you, and give you peace." There's that word "peace," one that many of us have shared numerous times. But have you ever considered the power of what it means? The last thing that your congregation hears in a service can potentially be the most important: It is being assured of God's peace.

I pray that you are continually aware of the "little things" in worship, ever mindful of the importance of God's blessing to us and the peace that God's blessing brings. When we are aware of the reality of God's peace in our lives, we can then bless others with both God's peace and our personal affirmation. Often, it is the little things in worship that make the greatest difference. The little word, "peace," and all that it includes is certainly one of those things.

Special Services

Enter His gates with thanksgiving and His courts with praise.
Give thanks to Him, bless His name.
(Ps. 100:4)

Prior to retiring from full-time ministry in 2015, I had the joy and privilege of working with many wonderful lay members in the congregations I served. In my last parish, I worked with one long-time member who had the responsibility of scheduling the lay readers for the various services. Boyd was well organized and conscientious about his job. He always had a "handle" on the Sunday morning services. However, he worried about the possibility of overlooking other worship times such as mid-week or festival services that were not included as part of the regular Sunday morning schedule.

Just to be sure that he was "on top of things," he would occasionally stop by my office, stand in the doorway, and ask, "Wally, do we have any special services coming up?" Every time, in response to his question, I would answer, "Boyd, they're *all* special!" He and I both laughed. Both of us knew exactly what the other was saying and thinking!

My purpose in sharing this story is to emphasize the truth that all of our worship services are special! We should never take our times of corporate worship for granted. What could be more special than gathering as the body of Christ and meeting the Lord face to face through all the elements of our worship?

The next time you may be tempted to think of your worship times as just one more thing to check off your "to do" list, remember how special the times in worship are. They are the times when you come into the Lord's presence and receive God's gifts to us, and in return you offer praise and thanks back to God.

The Realm of the Spirit

. . . be filled with the Spirit, speaking to one another in psalms and hymns and spiritual songs, singing and making melody with your heart to the Lord.
(Eph. 5:18-19)

On three different occasions I spent a week with the late Paul Christiansen, learning from him at his summer choral schools. Paul Christiansen was the son of F. Melius Christiansen, founder of the world-famous St. Olaf Choir. Paul was a renowned choral director in his own right at Concordia College in Moorhead, Minnesota for many years. Learning from a musical master like him was, and still is, one of the highlights of my musical training. He had a profound influence on my understanding and appreciation of sacred choral music and the choral art.

In addition to all the techniques and practices I learned during my time with Paul Christiansen, he often shared a short phrase that summarizes the motivation for serving the church through music: "Music has the power to lift us into the realm of the Spirit." Think about that for a moment. What you do on Wednesday or Thursday night and on Sunday morning with your choir is more than simply coming together and singing. What you prepare for and put into place with your choir is equipping them and your congregation to be taken into the very presence of the Spirit.

Think about Paul's quote. It goes hand in hand with what Martin Luther wrote: "Next to the Word of God, music deserves the highest praise." Why? Because it can, and does, take us into the realm of God's presence. The gift of music is not only a means to use in earthly worship, but it is also a gift from God that is present in heavenly worship. John's heavenly vision, as recorded in Revelation, affirms this fact: "And they sang a new song, saying, 'Worthy are You to take the book and to break its seals; for You were slain, and purchased for God with Your blood men from every tribe and tongue and people and nation'" (5:9).

Please do not misunderstand me. Music is not some sort of "magic carpet ride." Rather it is a divine gift given to us as a means to come before God with praise, worship, and thanksgiving for what he has done for us in Jesus.

As a worship leader and planner, you have the high calling of helping to lead others and transport your congregation and choir into the presence of the Lord. What you do is vitally important. It has eternal significance.

May your ministry and leadership be blessed by the Lord. May you draw upon the Lord to give you all you need as you help to take people into the "realm of the Spirit" through the gift of music.

What Do You Expect?

Behold, I tell you a mystery … we will all be changed.
(1 Cor. 15:51)

As a parent of two grown children, I still remember and think back to when they were very young. Many different events cross my mind, but one occurrence that stands out involved my daughter when she was about three years old. I don't recall exactly what she had done, but I do remember when I asked her about what had happened. Her response was unforgettable. With her little hand on her hip and a very serious look on her face, she replied to my question, "What do you 'ecpec?'" That's three-year-old language for "expect."

Perhaps you have heard the same answer when you have asked someone about their actions or words. "What do you expect?" Maybe it is an answer that should be asked when you think about what occurs in worship and what you hope to receive as a result of worship.

The answer likely varies from one person to another. One thing, though, is certain. When people come to worship, there is the opportunity for them to leave differently than when they came. When they arrive with a spirit of expectancy that God will do life-changing things, he will! "We know that when He appears, we will be like Him, because we will see Him just as He is" (1 John 3:2). Where God is present and individuals come in faith, people are changed. Sin is forgiven, faith is strengthened, relationships are restored, and prayers are answered. God is active!

A number of years ago the American hymnwriter Bryan Jeffery Leech wrote a text titled, "We Shall Be Changed," based on 1 Corinthians 15:51-52. While Bryan's specific text spoke to the resurrection and the second coming of Christ, his title can also speak to us as we enter worship. We shall be changed because we are meeting the resurrected Lord. This is a theological truth that lies at the very heart of all of the windows in this section dealing with "Worship That Transforms Lives."

What do you expect when you come to worship? Be ready to be different when you leave. Come to worship expecting God's touch upon your life. After all, "Christ is risen. He is risen indeed! Alleluia!"

How's the Health in Your Church?

"I say to you, get up, pick up your pallet and go home." And he got up and immediately
picked up the pallet and went out in the sight of everyone, so that they were all amazed
and were glorifying God, saying, "We have never seen anything like this."
(Mark 2:11-12)

Some people say that the church is a "hospital for sinners." The Gospels clearly show that much of Jesus' ministry was devoted to healing individuals of physical and emotional illness in addition to spiritual problems. Healing was a major part of his ministry.

If you have the important task of planning and leading worship, you spend a lot of time thinking about different parts of a service and those elements that will help individuals interact with God. You think about the music, the prayers, the proclamation of the Word, and times of fellowship. I wonder, however, how much time is dedicated to providing times within your worship when individuals have the opportunity to interact with Jesus and experience his various healings for them.

There is a risk of being so involved with thinking about the details of the next choir anthem or drama presentation, or if all the brass players you hired will show up, that you may neglect areas that deal with people in their hurts, pains, and illnesses. Making sure that the choir is prepared and that the brass instruments are tuned are important details. Far more important, though, is providing times when worshipers can receive every gift God has to offer in worship for the healing of our spirits and our bodies.

To provide opportunities in worship for individuals to experience God's healing power, consider including:

• A time for sharing God's peace among the worshipers, allowing for relationships to be restored
• A time for naming the sick out loud as you pray congregational prayers for healing
• A time for individual prayer with prayer counselors in the service, perhaps during Communion
• A time for confession and forgiveness, restoration and assurance

These are only some of the ways in which God's healing power can become a reality in the life of your congregation. Small steps such as these can lead to significant times of personal transformation. By affording individuals the chance to become vulnerable in worship, the spiritual health of one's congregation can see dramatic changes.

Worship That Changes People

. . . one thing I do know, that though I was blind, now I see.
(John 9:25)

There are many different ways of describing various age groups in today's culture. Pollsters often categorize people by their interests, education, and age—which some people would say is an attempt to further segment our society.

There is one area, however, that unifies all people regardless of age, interests, or education: worship. Everyone worships something. Harold Best has said it well: "Nobody does not worship."[2] Even individuals who make no claim to anything spiritual find themselves expressing great affection and devotion to someone or something. One needs to look no further than personal possessions or the entertainment industry.

Our purpose here, however, is to speak about those who, regardless of any group they have been "assigned to," are drawn to Christian worship. Those of us who help to shape and plan worship should ask: Do those in our congregation experience spiritual change in their lives when they worship? Does the hour they spend with the body of Christ give them the reality of God's forgiveness and life-changing love?

Perhaps you have asked yourself if your congregation has come to a place where they are simply going through the motions. Regardless of your worship style or tradition, there is always the danger of feeling as if nothing has happened in a service that impacts or helps the people you serve.

The need for people of all ages and cultural groups to be impacted by their encounter with the living God is real. Do not be satisfied in allowing people to go through worship without showing them the life-changing presence of God. As you begin to plan and prepare for worship, seek the Holy Spirit's guidance to direct you in his ways. Nothing would please Satan more than to have the church simply go through the motions. By the power and inspiration of the Holy Spirit, that danger can be negated.

Worship should be a life-changing experience. That change does not occur because of what is done in your own power. It happens because people recognize and experience what God wants to do for them as they meet him in the Word, the sacraments or ordinances, prayer, your expression of liturgy, contemplation, and whatever additional means the Holy Spirit chooses to reveal in worship.

Do those in your congregation recognize the presence and the power of our Father? Do they encounter and meet Jesus in a personal way? Are they filled with the life-giving breath of the Holy Spirit? These questions apply to everyone, regardless of age, gender, cultural setting, or denominational affiliation and tradition. These questions need to be continually considered as you plan and pray about the worship services you share with those you are called to serve.

Do You "Cense" God in Worship?

Another angel came and stood at the altar, holding a golden censer;
and much incense was given to him, so that he might add it to the prayers of all the saints
on the golden altar which was before the throne.
(Rev. 8:3)

I remember a time when I had the pleasure of attending the dedication of a beautiful pipe organ in a nearby Roman Catholic parish. The journey that this church had taken to get to their organ dedication took more than 20 years. You can imagine how thrilled they were. It was truly a festive occasion.

As part of the dedication service, there was a moment when the bishop moved before the organ and surrounded it with incense. Some denominations would not be comfortable with such a practice or would even consider it. In the Roman Catholic tradition, however, the use of incense is common and is used to set apart certain items for use in the worship of God. As the bishop was "censing the organ," the thought of how worshipers use all of their senses during worship crossed my mind.

Worship is not a spectator sport. Rather, it is an act that requires full participation. For some churchgoers, being present in a church on a Sunday morning during a service is their understanding of participating in worship. In some cases, attending is all they do. An individual does not worship by attending any more than a spectator plays in a football game while sitting on the sidelines. Worship requires us to focus on God with our sight and hearing. It also gives us the opportunity to use the senses of smell, touch, and taste.

Obviously, our vision and hearing present very clear ways in which we experience God in worship. The same may be said for our other senses when on certain occasions we can smell the incense being used, as we shake the hand of the person next to us in sharing the peace of God, and as we "taste and see that the Lord is good" during times of Holy Communion. Using all five senses gives us the opportunity to experience the fullness and richness of what is offered by the Lord in our corporate times of worship.

Perhaps you have noticed that I have mentioned nothing about the use of our voice in worship. It is difficult to imagine how we might experience corporate worship on a regular basis without the use of the important vehicle of our voice. As we consider the use of all of our senses in worship, we should give thanks for the variety of gifts God has given to us to worship him. One gift should not be overused at the expense of the others, however.

The Quakers use times of silence. The Orthodox include icons. Other traditions find the use of incense to be helpful. By being open to the many opportunities we have to use all of our senses, we acknowledge new possibilities and make ourselves available for God to reveal himself to us in new and meaningful ways.

Mountaintop Experiences

Six days later, Jesus took with Him Peter and James and John, and brought them up on a high mountain by themselves. And He was transfigured before them.
(Mark 9:2)

I suspect that you have heard the expression, "mountaintop experience," at one time or another. It is generally associated with feelings of excitement, joy, happiness, or some other emotion that deeply resonates in our heart. Perhaps you have heard it spoken by someone with respect to a particular worship service. It is not difficult to imagine hearing a person say, "That service was a mountaintop experience!" This experience would be the desired outcome rather than the "even though I walk through the valley" experiences.

We tend to equate mountaintop experiences with exuberance, and "valley" experiences with sadness and depression. There are, however, biblical examples where mountaintop experiences are more reflective and contemplative.

Throughout Scripture, there are examples of people being anything but joyous after meeting God on the mountain. Think of Moses and his initial meeting with God on the mountain. God had a specific plan. It was a time of great uncertainty for Moses, but a time that was ordained by God. It was a mountaintop experience.

Think of how Jesus took Peter, James, and John to the Mount of Transfiguration. That was a time of high drama. No doubt, the disciples came away from that event with great uncertainty about what they had witnessed. It, too, was a mountaintop experience.

Many years ago, my dear friend, Dr. William Lock, took several of us music ministers on a retreat high in the mountains. While there, he shared that he had been up very early in the morning and had gone to a quiet place to pray. He told us that the Lord had given him a word for each of us. What Bill shared with me that day has come true and has been a very important part of my life. He was not eager to share that word because he knew it would mean our friendship would be separated by many miles. His mountaintop experience was not one of great joy, but it was one where he met God and heard his voice.

Each of us have times when we interact with God on the mountain and he asks us to commune with him in quiet and reflective ways. Always remember that we are in the hands of a God who cares for us and knows us much better than we know ourselves. Having that faith and hope, each of us can go on in life without having all of the answers. That's a mountaintop experience!

Notes

Windows on Personal Devotion and Prayer

[1]Tony Campolo, "Hour of Power Message" (sermon, Crystal Cathedral, Garden Grove, CA, June 7, 2009), https://www.godtube.com/watch/?v=JC2JEMNU.

[2]Oswald Chambers, *My Utmost for His Highest* (Uhrichsville, OH: Barbour Books, 1963), October 11.

[3]Ibid., April 4.

[4]Thomas Ken, "Awake, My Soul, and with the Sun," (No. 868) in *Lutheran Service Book: Pew Edition* (St. Louis: Concordia Publishing House, 2006).

[5]Constance Cherry, "My House Shall Be Called a House of . . . Announcements," *Church Music Workshop* (January–April 2005): 3, 7, 8.

Windows on Reflections of Worship Theology and Practice

[1]Robert Webber, *Ancient-Future Worship* (Grand Rapids: Baker Books, 2008), 41.

[2]Rabanus Maurus, "Come, Holy Ghost, Creator Blest"(nos. 498 and 499) in *Lutheran Service Book: Pew Edition* (St. Louis: Concordia Publishing House, 2006).

[3]William Temple, *The Hope of a New World* (New York: MacMillan, 1942), 30.

[4]Evelyn Underhill, *Worship* (New York: Harper and Brothers, 1936), 3.

[5]Harold Best, *Music Through the Eyes of Faith* (San Francisco: Harper, 1993), 143.

[6]Anne Ortlund, *Up with Worship* (Nashville: Broadman and Holman, 2001), 44.

[7]The Commission on Worship of the Lutheran Church-Missouri Synod, *Lutheran Service Book: Pew Edition* (St. Louis: Concordia Publishing House, 2006), 164, 181.

Windows on Preparing for Worship

[1]Howard Stevenson, *Mastering Worship* (Portland, OR: Multnomah Press, 1990), 25.

Windows on Worship That Transforms Lives

[1]Carla Waterman, "Sacred Actions and Ministries of Worship" (lecture, Robert E. Webber Institute for Worship Studies, Orange Park, FL, June 17, 2003).

[2]Harold Best, *Unceasing Worship* (Downers Grove, IL: InterVarsity Press, 2003), 17.

Index of Biblical References

Mark

Luke

John

Acts

1 John

Revelation